MINDSCAPING

MINDSCAPING

A PRACTICAL GUIDE FOR
HOW TO BE HAPPIER

DONOVON JENSON

Paperback ISBN 978-1-7363507-0-6
Hardcover ISBN 978-1-7363507-2-0

www.howtohappy.com

Book design by G Sharp Design, LLC
www.gsharpmajor.com

CONTENTS

ABOUT THE AUTHOR

Donovon Jenson is a software engineer at Google, holding degrees in both health policy and psychology from the University of Utah. He is the author of *Surviving Customer Service* and *Real Resolutions.* Donovon teaches several courses, including Goal Setting Challenge and Happiness Challenge, each with over 3,000 students. He also runs the website How to Happy, which focuses on tools and information for optimizing happiness using psychologically sound principles. In his spare time, Donovon enjoys creating rap and poetry. He teaches courses on these subjects as well. His corresponding Youtube channel has had over 1.3 million views. You can contact him at howtohappy.com.

- https://www.instagram.com/thehowtohappy
- https://www.youtube.com/howtohappy
- https://www.linkedin.com/in/donovonjenson/

PREFACE

People's thoughts and actions have always fascinated me, and naturally, I was drawn to study psychology in college. Like most psych majors, I dabbled in cognition, clinical, social, personality, human factors, etc. Classes were interesting, but I never felt fully satisfied. I couldn't pin it down, but something was missing. We'll circle back to that...

During my senior year, life started to unravel. While there wasn't a single overwhelming or traumatic event, several stressors combined to erode my confidence and esteem. For the first time in my life, my next step wasn't planned. With graduation looming, the full existential weight of freedom came crashing down on me: *What am I supposed to do now? What is the point of all this? How do people live?* Added to this, my three-year romantic relationship was falling apart and my thesis was months behind.

It wasn't long before every waking moment was unpleasant. I felt worthless and directionless. I ramped up my relationship with alcohol and other recreational substances to numb my feelings. My college work was slipping, but I didn't care. I did only the minimum necessary. Each day was a struggle, with substance abuse staving off depressive thoughts just long enough to amplify them the next day. This bled into the rest of my life. I felt distant from friends and family, lacked empathy, and occasionally contemplated more powerful forms of escape, like harder drugs, leaving the country unannounced, suicide, etc. I went through the motions of life, miserable and uninspired. Nothing mattered. Nothing was interesting.

My response to seemingly standard or trivial problems may appear overblown. After all, I wasn't paralyzed, my family didn't die in a car accident, and I wasn't starving. I was graduating from college and experiencing a breakup. Life could have been much, much worse. Maybe this is why I didn't share how I was feeling with anyone. Pride also played its part. I studied psychology, after all, but I didn't make much progress. Each thought was an assault on my happiness. So, I escaped them however I could.

FINDING THE MISSING PIECE

My intention in telling this story isn't to elicit sympathy, but to explain my mental state at the beginning of my happiness journey. To explain that I don't have a natural disposition toward happiness. In fact, I come from a lineage ripe with predispositions to depression and anxiety.

The specific problems aren't important and are as real and debilitating as we allow them to be, regardless of the details. What is important is how unruly I allowed my mind to become. I had lost sight of what happiness was or how to create it.

That's what was missing from my education in psychology. We discussed plenty of theories, but few practical tools. Most information was far too context-specific and experimental, and so it was impossible to apply in daily life. I learned the mechanics of the mind, but almost nothing about how to improve my personal quality of life. Accordingly, I was unprepared to manage stress, rejection, pain, uncertainty, and negativity.

I was assigned a business book near the end of that year. As with the rest of my schoolwork, I only skimmed it enough to pass the test. By luck, a few concepts trickled through my hazy, substance-altered consciousness. The content was different than my psych texts—less theoretical, more immediate, and personal. One of the concepts eventually connected with my failed relationship: "We can emotionally manage more when we realize others are not objects to fulfill our desires, but individuals with their own desires. Try looking at others in this way."

I wondered: *Could this apply to me?* The way I framed the relationship repeatedly caused pain. I always planned quality time, bought gifts, and was emotionally supportive. *She was supposed to reciprocate. Instead, she acted like it meant nothing. How could she? What is the point of investing in relationships?* I saw the relationship as a transaction. What did she want? Primarily, someone with similar religious beliefs.

That wasn't me. Her lack of desire to continue the relationship had nothing to do with my worth or investment in the relationship. That realization alone didn't fix my mindset, but it certainly helped—one breath of fresh air in a toxic mental landscape. I finally felt some relief. That's when the momentum shifted. I stumbled upon another book, and another useful idea tumbled out:

....

Focusing on events outside your
control only leads to frustration. Focus
only on what you can influence.

....

I finally saw a path to restoring balance in my life. I needed more exposure to practical information regarding relationships, happiness, productivity, and mental health. Resources focused on action and results, not just the mind's structure.

I developed a list of generally well-regarded self-help, philosophy, communication, and practical psychology books. Finally seeing a path forward, consuming information became a priority. The process produced mixed results. Many resources were insightful. Others were misguided, confusing, and potentially harmful as some mixed illogical frameworks with useful exercises and vice versa. I oscillated between intrigue and frustration, parsing out what seemed both plausible and valuable.

Over the next few years, I experimented with a range of tools from varying disciplines. I explored adding variants of "happiness habits" to my routine, zealously testing for efficacy. I created my own life plan with meaningful goals instead of trying to figure out what was expected of me. Life kept improving. The steps became clearer. For the first time in years, I believed I could be happier.

I wrote a book about a personal goal-setting experiment, then turned the associated insights into a course. I started writing blog posts about happiness, interviewing others, and reviewing the books I read. I created another course based on those insights.

I still spend a large percentage of my time consuming, trying, and distilling happiness-based content. I regularly test ideas and tools against practical, logical filters to parse what's most sensical. This book is my attempt at extracting the high-level insights I have gained and presenting them in a practical, straightforward framework.

WHAT'S IN IT FOR YOU?

This book is designed to guide you through the process of creating a lifelong happiness-optimization process. It contains practical ideas, and each section includes specific exercises, but the framework is meant to be generalizable. You should be able to use it to determine how other resources impact your happiness as well.

Below is a visual overview of the key mindscaping concepts. Each major theme mirrors landscaping in some way. In essence, it is simply a cyclical process of surveying, planning, and executing. In practice, however, knowing the details and nuances of this process is important. A framework makes it far easier to conceptually package your thoughts, actions, and intentions toward happiness.

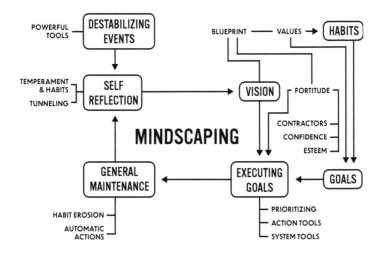

Treating happiness this way may seem restrictive or technical, but having the vocabulary to accurately describe your experiences makes it easier to optimize. A framework clarifies what aspects of life are currently most relevant to your happiness. This streamlines your attention, generating results more quickly. Ideally, you spend more time fulfilled or working toward it and less time wondering what to do next.

Disappointing as it may be, this book won't provide an instant cure. Nothing exists at such a broad level, even for marketing purposes. Instant unshakable happiness, a perfect, problem-free life, and infinite productivity aren't realistic goals. There are no shortcuts to a meaningful, pleasant life. It takes time and effort. I can, however, confidently say that channeling effort through this framework produces tangible increases in happiness over time. It is a logical process for identifying, adjusting, and developing positive habits that produce happiness. Everything else gets cut out. You can't be happy all the time, but you can absolutely be happy more often.

This book is my best attempt at condensing years of knowledge and experimentation into an approachable, concise package. It is designed to help you find a range of valuable techniques for improving happiness, and my hope is that you'll find something valuable here, regardless of your life circumstances.

1

THE HAPPINESS FRAMEWORK

Imagine standing near the edge of a cliff overlooking two landscapes. On one side, the sun radiates golden rays across a verdant valley. Clusters of lush gardens and massive trees are visible for miles. Elegant pathways interweave the greenery, leading to features such as a tennis court, gazebo, and cabin, to name a few. You can just make out a shimmering blue lake, complete with a dock, off in the distance.

In the center of this landscape lies what can only be described as a modern castle. Massive pillars laced with gold decorate an imposing structure. Intricate, colorful designs snake their way up the walls. Near the entrance is a perfectly manicured lawn, a massive fountain trickling in the center. Everything has been meticulously kept. The view is breathtaking.

You can barely look away, especially compared to the other side of the valley. It roughly mirrors the first landscape, but in an unsettling and uncanny way. It is a wasteland: chaotic, random, and overrun with weeds. Muddy paths haphazardly zigzag in incomprehensible patterns, seemingly leading nowhere. The corresponding lake is more of a murky, brown swamp.

The building in the center of this landscape is so small it's hardly visible. From what you can make out, it is a dingy, unstable shack made of cardboard and planks. It appears as though it might collapse at any moment. Glass is scattered everywhere, presumably from what were once windows. Huge chunks of the walls are torn down, exposing the interior to the elements. It's also confusingly placed. No pathways lead there. You could walk right by and never notice.

Which landscape would you rather live in? It's barely worth asking. The answer is clear. Yet, many of us allow our minds to exist much like the second, disheveled landscape. Without knowing how to shape our mental landscapes, many fall into disrepair. This metaphor may not be clear yet, but in the following chapters, we will explore how the mind is like a landscape, why that's useful knowledge, and how you can optimize happiness by maintaining your mind like a piece of property.

CORE HAPPINESS QUESTIONS

In my journey to understand the mind, countless questions have arisen. Digging into topic-specific resources answered many of them. Unfortunately, happiness wasn't one of those topics. I found some useful bits and pieces, but no single resource comprehensively explained how I should live to be happiest. I particularly struggled with the following three questions:

WHAT IS HAPPINESS AND WHY IS IT SO ELUSIVE?

Most resources don't even bother trying to define happiness. Others felt vague. Is it pleasure? Satisfaction? Contentment? Being in the moment? What do *those* mean? When can someone say they are experiencing happiness? When two people say, "I'm happy," do they mean the same thing?

WHY IS THERE SO MUCH CONFLICTING INFORMATION ON HAPPINESS?

There are volumes of conflicting advice. Some claim religion is the only route to happiness, while others claim happiness comes from not being religious. Others say religion is irrelevant, and happiness is actually rooted in relationships. Are some individuals born happy and others miserable? What are the variables?

Even smaller, specialized tools can be confusing. One expert touts positive thinking as the answer to stress. Another says positive thinking doesn't help at all. One guru says hypnosis is key for health, another one says it's time in nature. The results are inconsistent as well. One method works marvelously for half the population and fails for the rest. Are they implementing the tools incorrectly? Are people lying about the results? Why are happiness tools so inconsistent? What actually works?

WHAT ACTIONS OPTIMIZE HAPPINESS?

Learning how the mind works can be helpful, but how can we actually produce happiness? Ideas aren't useful without knowing how to implement them. Phrases like "choose to be happy," "let happiness find you," and "be happy in the present" may appear meaningful but are hollow upon further inspection. How do we live these platitudes? If happiness was one simple choice, we would have all made it by now.

Yet, I've seen these phrases repeated and spouted as pillars of sound advice. For those struggling with happiness, it is not only unhelpful but also detrimental. *Happiness should come easily. What's wrong with me? It's my fault for not letting happiness find me.* Are most individuals broken, or is the advice too naive? How, exactly, can we consistently increase happiness? What's an approachable but actionable framework?

These three questions and their corollaries have racked my brain for years. After countless hours of research, contemplation, and trials, I've finally refined satisfactory answers. In this book, I'll guide you through my exploration of these questions. It takes time to fully unpack the details, but by the end, you should have a comprehensive answer to the question: What is happiness, and how do I optimize it?

FRAMING THE FRAMEWORK

I want to start by answering the previous questions. These answers are complex but provide a baseline for exploring the mind and happiness. Conceptually, this is the most challenging part of the book, and using mindscaping only requires understanding the broad, high-level points. If you find some nuances or psychological jargon hard to follow, I recommend continuing forward anyway. Subsequent chapters are far easier to comprehend and also more practical.

1. DEFINING HAPPINESS

Our first task is normalizing a definition of happiness from first principles, starting with a fairly safe premise: If happiness means anything at all, it's desirable and preferable to being unhappy. There are ways we prefer to exist and ways we'd rather not experience. This seems intuitive, even if we don't have metrics for distinguishing between these preferences yet.

There is a vast range of possible experiences and no clear metrics for when experiences switch from happy to unhappy. Tasks like buying groceries seem to fall somewhere in the neutral zone. With that in mind, it's reasonable to assume preferable states exist on a spectrum instead of being binary. That is to say, experiences aren't absolute bliss or complete dejection. Getting a massage is preferable to coughing, which is more preferable than being hit by a car. At a certain level of desirability, most of us label those experiences as "happiness."

It also seems clear that we can only determine the desirability of a state if we're aware of it. Most of us are familiar with the experience of noticing a small cut sometime after it happened. When we notice it, it starts to hurt. Yet, it was bleeding the whole time. Neurons were firing. We just weren't directing attention to the injury. Without attention, the experience never entered our consciousness, even though the signals were there.

Here's an exercise to illustrate. Focus your attention on the sensation of your feet. Now shift to your hearing. Now to your breath. By shifting your focus, you'll notice different aspects of your physical experience. These channels constantly generate information, but you only notice what you tune into. If an event isn't in your awareness, you can't determine how desirable it is. In the same way, we must be conscious to focus attention on an event and evaluate how desirable it is. Without consciousness, there is no experience. It's hard to argue we're happy or unhappy while asleep or in a coma (unless semi-consciousness is granted, like during dreams). We may judge the desirability of the state later when we're conscious, but during the experience itself, we can't evaluate its desirability. Happiness is only relevant when processing experiences.

We can now reasonably say that happiness is dependent on the ability to evaluate the desirability of a particular experience. Yet, consciousness and attention don't necessitate evaluation. We can become fully immersed in activities without any awareness of happiness or even ourselves. The clearest example is when your attention is completely consumed by a task—often called "psychological flow" or "being in the zone."

When we're completely engaged—the moment we're catching a ball, projecting a bird's flight path, or practicing piano—we're neither happy nor unhappy. Attention is consumed by the act itself. We don't have spare capacity to evaluate states for desirability. We only experience happiness relative to these activities, which requires attention.

This may appear to be misleading or untrue. You might think: *I get frustrated when losing a game,* or *I feel excited when reciting a song perfectly.* While it may seem like you are focusing and feeling simultaneously, there are actually small gaps between the moments of your attention. To explain, we need to lean on research. Current multitasking experiments suggest the prefrontal cortex, which controls attention, can only hold a single focus. They have also found it can take a few hundred milliseconds to switch focus.

This can be seen clearly in a well-established experiment where individuals are asked to locate a particular letter or number in a series of characters. Flashing characters too rapidly causes complete misses in detection, referred to as attentional blink. At a certain point, we simply can't switch our focus fast enough to complete the task.

This means we can't actually focus on multiple tasks at the exact same time, only rapidly switch our attention. Since we can't split our focus, experiencing frustration or joy during an event means we've momentarily changed our focus to process desirability. It can feel like focusing on an event and evaluating it happen simultaneously, but they don't. Millisecond switching costs aren't long enough to be noticeable.

You might be able to recognize the truth of this by considering intense moments. As the intensity rises, states demand more attention, which limits switching. For example, at a certain level of pain, the feeling consumes your attention. If you have an absolutely crushing migraine, you'll feel neither happy nor unhappy because you'll be focused on the event itself. When even minute attention is freed, it will almost certainly be evaluated negatively, but that requires a switch.

Another example is dealing with danger, such as a deer running out in front of your car. All your attention shifts to navigating the situation, not evaluating it. Only later, in evaluation, can you determine how happy or unhappy you were in those moments. It's also why we can "blackout" when emotions are too strong. All attention cycles are consumed or overwhelmed by emotion, leaving no space for self-evaluation.

This is what determines whether we experience happiness during an event. If you spend even a few attention cycles evaluating states, you may perceive emotion and focus as existing simultaneously. If not, you won't feel happy or unhappy about the event until later evaluation.

With these mechanics outlined, let's craft a definition.

....

Happiness is how desirable states are during moments of evaluation.

....

This still feels more theoretical than practical. Plus, half the terms are unclear. Let's extract more layers until we discover a more relatable and intuitive definition.

2. WHAT ARE DESIRABLE STATES?

Let's start the cleanup process by refining the definition of a state. We've established there is a spectrum of desirable experiences, but what does that mean? What are you evaluating? What constitutes a state?

The simplest entry point is subdividing states into more granular categories of experience. One clear type of experience is physical. Physical sensations may be related to other experiences, but they have a distinct quality. Eating, breaking your leg, kissing, tiredness, stretching, and itching are all examples of physical sensations that vary in desirability and intensity.

Emotions are another distinct type of experience. While there's often interconnection with physical states, we'd never confuse knee pain with joy. In addition, research shows different parts of the brain are responsible for each type of experience. Feelings like comfort, frustration, fear, confusion, sadness, and others fall under this umbrella. Again, each varies in intensity and desirability.

The last distinct type of experience is thought. Thoughts are pieces of information, which may or may not be grounded in reality or coherency. They can be produced by the brain, external stimuli, or evaluations. While it's possible to further subdivide thought production with substantial nuance, this covers what's important for mindscaping without exploring unnecessary complexity.

Instead, let's streamline the discussion by focusing on how thoughts are evaluated for desirability. Most commonly, this is done by evaluating thoughts and actions for their meaning. That is to say, we ask ourselves *how desirable is my relationship with this information?* This is also complicated because our relationship with any particular thought or experience is completely subjective.

Take a thought like: *I am ugly.* Most people's relationship with this thought creates a fairly negative evaluation: *I hate my appearance.* But there are many other possible relationships, such as *Being ugly makes me unique,* or *My brain just created that thought. It's not true. I feel comfortable with my appearance*—both of which are far more desirable.

Meaning is self-produced. The easiest way to think about optimizing this state is by considering it as purpose or meaning. Aligning your thoughts and actions with your values generally produces desirable relationships. Getting promoted, publishing a book, and getting married are a few among countless examples. While focusing on purpose doesn't cover your relationship with all possible thoughts, it encapsulates what produces the majority of results. It's also much more approachable than trying to consider all possible forms of thought and how they interconnect.

One last caveat to consider is projected states, which are not grounded in immediate sensations or experiences. Instead, they're projected from either the past, the future, or they are entirely imagined. Technically, these projections are also thoughts and are evaluated accordingly.

One example is thinking about public speaking, then evaluating that thought as unpleasant. The speech itself isn't unpleasant, because you haven't experienced it yet. The imagined projection of how the event will be is what's unpleasant. Another example is thinking nostalgically about an unpleasant childhood event. It was unpleasant at the time, but a projection with a new frame of nostalgia can make it pleasant now. Neither projection is based in reality but in subjective perception.

Projections won't be extracted as a separate state since they add substantial complexity, and optimizing thoughts for purpose improves most projections. Projections are, however, something to be aware of while becoming more familiar with your thoughts. Many people spend significant time evaluating projections in a way that decreases their happiness, becoming lost in the past, future, or imaginary counterfactuals. This is common enough that it's worth mentioning, but not distinct enough to warrant further discussion in considering how best to optimize happiness.

3. OPTIMIZING HAPPINESS STATES

The nuances of state evaluation can be difficult to follow. The simple version is:

....

Focus on optimizing three states— the physical, emotional, and purposeful to optimize happiness.

....

Optimizing these three states narrows your focus to the factors that most impact happiness. However, we still have a prioritization problem. What if optimizing two states creates a conflict? Should we do something meaningful if it's physically painful? What if something purposeless creates desirable emotional states? In this section, we'll explore an optimization hierarchy.

Balancing purpose, emotional pleasure, and physical pleasure is no simple task. Individual happiness is delicate, and it's certainly more artistic than formulaic. That being said, we can still rationalize a few preferences during conflicts. Some states tend to weigh more heavily than others during evaluations.

Imagine being the best, happiest, most fulfilled version of yourself. Now consider how you would resolve competing state choices. Let's start with physical and emotional pleasure. Would you accept anxiety and anger in exchange for good food and massages? How about delicious smells in exchange for permanent loneliness? For states with roughly equivalent intensities, the answer is clear: emotional states trump physical ones.

Comparing emotional states against purpose is more difficult, but remember you're making these decisions as your best, happiest self. Trading emotional states for purposeful ones are common. We work long, stressful hours to provide for our families. We bore ourselves studying to earn degrees. We care for sick children even while they vomit on us. These activities are unpleasant at the time, yet most of us decide they are worthwhile trade-offs.

We often see the opposite as well, however. The person who is fearful of rejection, for example, avoids applying for a promotion or asking out a romantic interest. Skipping these opportunities to avoid feeling discomfort is common, but are these decisions made by your ideal, happiest self?

Unlikely. These trades generally create long-term regret, which is itself an undesirable state. Sacrificing purpose now can provide immediately desirable emotional states but is likely to cost you greater purpose and emotional pleasure later. Overall, a net loss in happy moments. Accordingly, it's also a poor strategy for optimizing happiness. At equivalent intensities, purpose tends to trump emotional pleasure.

Based on these comparisons, we now have a ranking. States should be preferred in the following order, assuming intensity is relatively the same:

1. Purpose
2. Emotional pleasure
3. Physical pleasure

You may be wondering why I keep mentioning equal intensity. To explain, imagine the following trade-offs. Would you help someone cross the street for 14 billion years of agonizing pain? How about being permanently isolated in a vacuum in exchange for five seconds of feeling excited? At a certain point, the intensity of an experience's desirability is more important than its type. Our typical daily situation is far less intense, so the rule of thumb generally applies.

This also explains why we shouldn't focus on one state at the exclusion of others. Let's say providing for your family is meaningful to you. You can do this by undertaking backbreaking, frustrating work. This creates desirable purpose states, but undesirable emotional and physical states.

Yes, it creates some level of happiness, but would you say it's your best life? Is it optimized for happiness? Probably not. You might be willing to sacrifice emotional and physical pleasure to provide for your family, but is such a sacrifice always absolutely necessary? What if there was a way to make the same income, but through more desirable physical and emotional states? While it may take time and effort to discover and transition, such a path typically exists.

With this information in mind, we can now generate a generic formula for optimizing happiness.

....

When there is a conflict between states of equivalent intensities, optimize for purpose, then emotional pleasure, then physical pleasure. If there are no conflicts, optimize each state as much as possible.

....

While this is only a rough guideline, it optimizes for happiness in most situations. We'll cover how to do this in subsequent chapters.

PRESENT PAYMENT FOR FUTURE STATES

Another consideration in optimizing happiness is balancing conflicts between present and future happiness. Should you choose desirable states now at the cost of derailing the future? Or invest now for improved returns later? The difficulty of this choice is compounded by our inability to predict the future. We can make plans, but life can change drastically at any moment.

Here's an example of a potential conflict. Let's say you have $5,000 today. Is it better to take a vacation or save for a house? Will you experience more happiness using the money now, or investing and increasing it?

Unfortunately, there's no straightforward answer. The situation's full context makes a huge difference, and educated guesses will always be part of the formula. We can, however, use the happiness concepts we've explored so far to compare choices.

- → Which is more meaningful to you, the experience of a vacation or owning a home?
- → How much faster can you purchase a home by investing the $5,000?
- → What states do you expect from vacationing?
- → How long do you expect them to last?
- → What states do you expect from owning a home?
- → How long do you expect those to last?

There are no right answers. It depends on your position, the likely outcomes, and your priorities. Your personal experience and values heavily color the preferable decision here. Even then, it might be a tough choice. Not all present/future decisions are this hard, though. Sometimes thinking in terms of states and correlated evaluations makes the preferred decision clear.

For example, let's say you're already somewhat sick from binging on sweets and eyeing another cookie. Is it worth it? Let's think in terms of desirable states, specifically regarding length. Eating the cookie may provide up to a minute of enjoyment. What's the cost? More hours of higher intensity physical discomfort from overeating. Plus, the negative health impacts of extra sugar and calories. The preferred choice here seems straightforward.

It's easy when looking at hypotheticals and thinking of your best self. In reality, taking action is harder than simply knowing the preferable choice at a distance. It requires recognizing the situation in the moment, determining the optimal decision, and overcoming conflicting impulses. We'll increase granularity on those details later. For now, present-future conflicts are often much easier when considered in terms of their impact on states and evaluations.

ALTERING EVALUATIONS

Optimizing states is useful, but it is only half the equation. Happiness is also dependent on how you evaluate your relationship with a particular state. While some states are more desirable than others, evaluations can drastically modify the final result. Optimization can shift the ratio in our favor, but undesirable states are an inevitable part of the human experience. Evaluations are the only factor we always control to some degree. An evaluation has two components:

1. Framing
2. Focus

FRAMING

Framing is your perceived relationship with the experience. For example, feeling pain from a workout could be framed as: *My body can't handle this, I'm pushing myself extra hard today,* or *I'm such a weakling.* Each state has an infinite number of possible frames, with varying degrees of desirability. Different frames are how identical experiences can produce different levels of happiness.

Frames are anchored in your upbringing, experience, and education. Reframing in the moment is not a natural skill for most of us and requires an acute awareness of your thoughts, plus the knowledge of alternatives and the open-mindedness to adopt them. Occasionally, new information will cause a drastic shift in frames. More often, however, it requires repeated exposure to the new frame paired with practice catching, challenging, and replacing the less useful frame. We'll discuss how this is done in subsequent chapters.

FOCUS

You can also influence your focus, changing the state you choose to evaluate. For example, a thought like *I'm not attractive* may cross your mind. Focus determines how much attention that thought receives. You can choose to look for evidence that the thought is true, reasons it's untrue, or tune into your breath. The thought could last a second, or you could deepen, strengthen, and repeat it until it ruins your entire day. Developing the skill of controlling your focus more reliably reduces the duration of unavoidable, unpleasant states.

We don't, however, have exclusive control over attention. Our brain does significant processing outside of consciousness, some of which can force attention toward certain stimuli. Consider loud, unexpected sounds. You don't choose to focus on them. Instead, the brain region responsible for digesting auditory information says: *Something potentially important is happening. Pay attention to this now in case you need to respond.*

As state intensity increases, so do the demands on focus. Consider breaking a bone or having a panic attack. Redirecting attention is exponentially more difficult in these instances. These states have serious potential consequences, so attention hijacking is warranted. We can't overwrite this system, and if we could, it would be dangerous. Luckily, everyday states are low intensity and far more susceptible to influence.

Our aim then is to become aware of our thoughts and evaluations, intercepting them as they arise. Instead of mindlessly exploring a thread like *I'm worthless*, we increase the distance between thought and evaluation so we can choose more desirably. We can interject ideas such as *That was just a thought, I'm choosing another focus* instead of ones like *Knowing I'm worthless reminds me that I should give up*. Again, how to do this will become clearer as we progress.

USING THIS INFORMATION EFFECTIVELY

At this point, we have crafted a robust definition of happiness and a few rough optimizations. While still fairly abstract, we've explored the core concepts. The rest of the book explains a practical framework for increasing the desirability of states and evaluations. Nuanced complexity inherently missing from such a broad definition is intermixed as needed throughout subsequent chapters.

At a high level, mindscaping is a cyclical process of reflecting, planning, acting, and evaluating. The aim is to increase the frequency and intensity of desirable states and evaluations, which increases happiness accordingly. Executing this process consistently produces tangible changes in experience, especially over time.

STRATEGY OVER TACTICS

There are a few additional concepts you'll likely find useful before diving into the mindscaping process. Let's start by exploring the distinction between strategy and tactics. You may already have an idea, but we'll cover the definitions for clarity.

Strategy is the overarching plan used to accomplish a goal. It's a high-level, all-encompassing approach. Strategy is the grand vision, the master plan, for what you're aiming to bring into the world. If you're writing a book, then the strategy would be plot and purpose, the cohesive structure. If you were trying to get in shape, the strategy might be weightlifting. It's a general, broad approach.

Tactics are the specific actions taken to execute a strategy, and there are usually many available options. Tactics are detailed, actionable, and specific. In writing a book, tactics might be a specific word choice or grammar style. For fitness, tactics could be individual exercises chosen to construct workouts. They are the more granular implementation steps.

Consider the goal of reducing muscle tension. You might choose relaxation as a strategy. The tactics of stretching or massage could be used to implement this strategy. Both tactics lead to increased physical relaxation, accomplishing the goal of reducing muscle tension. Neither is preferable at face value. At an individual level, however, I might prefer massage while stretching works better for you.

If both produce strategically equivalent results, the tactics are essentially interchangeable.

This explains why happiness advice is often conflicting. Many resources confuse tactics for strategy or see them as inseparable. If you believe one tactic is the only way to fulfill a strategy, that's what you'll advocate for. This doesn't work at scale. We're each wired differently. Effective tactics vary by individual.

Accordingly, I've focused on honing a generalizable strategy for optimizing happiness. While we'll also cover broadly effective tactics, these are for the sake of example and ease of implementation. There are countless additional possibilities. If the tactics I've selected don't fit your exact circumstances, search for others that will help you to implement the same strategy. The strategy for optimizing happiness is far more important than individual tactics.

A METAPHOR FOR APPROACHABILITY

Many happiness-related resources are densely packed with useful information. Unfortunately, many lack clear or memorable ways to organize those concepts. In the same vein, you may have trouble remembering the happiness concepts we've already discussed. So, to make the mindscaping framework more digestible, I've constructed it around the metaphor of the mind as a landscape. This makes the ideas easier to explain and remember. While not essential to the core concepts, imagery helps clarify nebulous ideas. It also provides a convenient shorthand for speaking about complex concepts.

Landscapes, however, are not a perfect 1:1 model of the mind. Not all sections, particularly tactical details, will be tied back into the metaphor. The metaphor supplements the core concepts by providing strategic guideposts and similar mental models. It doesn't, however, carry the full weight and details of all the information contained in this book. Don't expect perfect synchronicity.

Finally, strategies and tactics don't create change by themselves. You must take action to see results. We'll explore generally effective tools, but no tool can absolve you of responsibility for acting. Only you can choose to go to bed earlier or show compassion. Only you can apply for a better job. Only you can begin a mindfulness practice to better manage emotions. The framework helps, but the execution is entirely in your hands.

2

THE MIND AS A LANDSCAPE– THE MENTAL ECOSYSTEM

Optimizing happiness requires understanding how the mind functions. It may feel like states and happiness are solely determined by events the world thrusts upon you. In reality, however, you can influence or control many significant factors. In most situations external events play a minor role compared to your habitual reactions and frames.

Every event creates an impulse, sensation, or state. You then frame your relationship to that experience, which determines not only its desirability but the next action as well. Impulses vary in strength based on each individual and their circumstances. For example, seeing a leaf may produce a weak impulse to pick it up. You may frame that as *What would I do with a leaf?* Then choose the action of leaving it on the ground. The process isn't always completely conscious, but it follows a general pattern. Event, impulse, evaluation, action.

Now imagine relaxing on a warm beach, enjoying the sunshine, listening to soft ocean sounds. You're completely calm and half-asleep when a dog runs by dragging its leash. Moments later, a child follows, chasing the dog. As they pass, the kid kicks up a small whirlwind of sand, covering your eyes, nose, mouth, towel, and beach bag. What impulses, frames, and reactions might that elicit for you? And how strongly?

There are many possibilities. You might feel a strong impulse of anger. What a careless child! You might react by yelling, fuming, or chasing them. Your evaluation might be discomfort framed by empathy: *Sand is annoying, but it's just a child. It was an accident.* You might feel annoyed without an empathetic frame. *This is stinging my eyes, and I have to clean out my bag now. So frustrating!* The state here is exactly the same, but our impulses, frames, and reactions heavily dictate our subsequent evaluations and reactions.

These impulses, frames, and reactions aren't bound to your personality traits. It's not that I'm grouchy and you're nice, that's how we were born and how we'll always be. Instead, your beliefs, choices, and experiences form habits. Those habits largely determine which impulses, frames, and reactions are most likely to arise. These habitual thoughts and responses are modifiable to a major degree.

Take tripping, for example. Extending your hand to brace against falling is a natural impulse. Without training, this impulse might be incredibly powerful. It's likely the response you'd choose, with an automatic framing: *This might hurt my hand but will save my face.* Yet, we're also capable of overriding this impulse and rewriting the frame. With enough notice, intention, and practice, we can consciously choose a different frame: *Three of my fingers are broken, my shoulder will take the impact better than my hand.*

You could also train yourself not to extend your hand. With enough conscious repetition, the impulse could be modified to signal you to retract your arm instead of extending it. Your default behavior would shift. What seems like an inherent, mandatory response can be transformed by dedicated effort.

This is true of most reactions. When sand is kicked in your face, anger is your likely default. Framing the event negatively could create more anger, leading to an aggressive response like yelling. You can, however, train yourself to notice and weaken these impulses, enhance frames, and choose more relaxed responses. We'll discuss the specifics later. For now, focus on your capacity to influence impulses, reactions, and frames.

You only control some subset of factors for any given event. Determining exactly what you can control or at least influence becomes critical. This may sound trivial, but we often err too far in one direction. At the extremes, this appears as helplessness, remorse, and frustration. Focusing on a factor beyond your control will always be fruitless.

Take getting cut off in traffic as an example. This event is out of our control. What we do control, however, is the frame. We can choose to respond with *How careless!* Or with *Perhaps they didn't see me.* This frame will make a big difference in our subsequent response.

....

You can't control every event, but you can control your subsequent steps.

....

Now imagine deciding between a burger and a pizza for lunch. You decide on pizza, but when it arrives, you're disappointed by the taste. Considering what is in your control, you think: *I shouldn't have picked this. I wish I made the other choice.* This seems rational but is slightly misguided.

You're thinking about an event you controlled in the past. After making a decision, it's irreversible. Considering counterfactuals, especially for long periods, misdirects your attention. That choice is gone. You only control future decisions, so a frame like *Next time, I'll pick the burger* is far more useful.

We control a substantial portion of our life experience at every level, from daily decisions to lifelong milestones. We can choose a smaller city. We can look for a better job. We can join a club. It all relies on analyzing problems, determining what we control, and taking action. Curating your mind in this way tunes it for efficiency, causing it to seek out places where effort makes a difference.

The alternative is letting the world decide. This means existing by happenstance, passively allowing the past to dictate the future. Leaving it to chance generally produces unhappiness. Fortunately, we can also intentionally select a future direction, determine what we control, and work toward it. With happiness as an intention, we're far more likely to succeed.

This means you are largely responsible for your own happiness. Choices matter. Effort counts. It also means we're all empowered to increase happiness, regardless of what life has dealt us. We can all optimize further, no matter who you are, where you're from, or what you've done.

....

Each of us can labor to align our impulses, frames, and actions with desirable states.

....

WHY A LANDSCAPE?

This leads to my metaphor: the mindscape. There are many parallels between optimizing happiness and beautifying terrain. By thinking about your mind like a landscape, it's easier to understand the change process in an intuitive way. Landscapes also provide clear layers of abstraction. This mirrors the concepts we'll cover well, starting strategically then shifting tactically. Moving forward, imagine every individual mind as a unique landscape—a *mindscape*. Each mindscape has the following attributes:

- ➜ A relatively large piece of land (at least fifty acres).
- ➜ The land is owned, maintained, and lived on by one person (whoever's mind it is).
- ➜ There are natural features (e.g., trees, lakes, rivers, shrubs, hills, rocks, etc.).
- ➜ There are also man-made features (e.g., paths, sheds, fountains, etc.).
- ➜ There is a shelter or other form of housing on the property.
- ➜ The landscape is subject to normal change processes (i.e., hills erode, trees grow, etc.).
- ➜ Natural disasters, like tornadoes and floods, are possible.

The importance of these attributes may not be clear yet. That will change as we continue. Attributes are mainly introduced here to synchronize what we imagine, since mindscaping consumes the rest of the book. With that in mind, let's further explore the parallels between minds and landscapes.

NO TWO MINDSCAPES ARE IDENTICAL

All landscapes are unique, even if they share common features. Some landscapes have clearly distinct elements. For example, tundras are cold with short growing seasons, while rainforests have heavy precipitation and massive trees. Yet, even equivalent types of landscapes have unique compositions. Two rainforests might contain similar trees, but they won't be distributed exactly the same. They'll both have rainfall, but the average may differ significantly. One might be younger, with relatively shorter trees. Another might be severely damaged because of a natural disaster.

We can make generalizations, but we can't precisely predict individual elements. That means we must treat each landscape on a case-by-case basis. You couldn't say, "I've been to one forest, I know where to find the biggest tree in every forest now." Knowing the features provides useful information, but you still need to learn the details of each location to know it intimately.

Minds work similarly. We share similarities, but to truly understand an individual's mind, we must explore the nuances. For example, two individuals may struggle with controlling their temper. While the challenge may feel similar, it can produce entirely different responses. Maybe one becomes physically aggressive while another disengages. Perhaps these impulses are far stronger for one of them. One may frame their anger as useful, the other frightening. These differences drastically impact our experience as well as our ability to understand others effectively.

This also means individuals often use similar words to describe different experiences. These differences are anchored to their particular mindscape. The largest tree in your environment might be thirty feet, while in mine, it's only five feet. Your sadness might create stronger impulses than mine, in a way I've never experienced. Sometimes our approximations are close enough, other times large gaps in communication form. In speaking about individual experience, clarifying questions are essential.

Even so, we can't eliminate all discrepancies. We are all unique, with different experiences and genetic compositions. We can never perfectly understand someone else's mind. Accordingly, we must remain flexible about our beliefs of others' minds. Shared experience and psychological shortcuts can be helpful, but overgeneralization inevitably creates incorrect assumptions.

Likewise, other people can't perfectly navigate your mind either. They may know you well enough to predict thoughts and actions, but they can't know your precise experience of the world. You alone experience your life. This may feel isolating, but we can approximate well enough to connect with others. The point here is that learning about another individual comes with many layers of depth. Making nuanced assumptions about specific minds is likely to be wrong.

CLIMATE AND FEATURES: TEMPERAMENT AND HABITS

Many landscape attributes are modifiable, but others don't budge much. For example, we may not know the exact volume, but all rainforests experience frequent rain. It's an inherent part of the climate and not amenable to change. Features, however, are highly modifiable. Consider cacti, which might grow easily in a desert. That doesn't mean they exist in a particular desert. We could, however, plant them there. In your mind, climate and features work like temperament and habits.

Temperament is your mindscape's climate: your inborn, baseline traits. Certain attributes and predispositions can't be altered. For example, a certain segment of the population will always be more prone to depression, regardless of their actions. It's part of the way their mind is constructed. That doesn't mean it's inevitable, just that they may need to optimize happiness around this factor. Another group may need to optimize happiness around dyslexia. Baselines don't determine outcomes, but they do dictate some parts of our experience.

As with the cacti, climate determines which features thrive in a particular landscape. For example, we could remove every tree in a rainforest or create a lake in the desert. It wouldn't be easy, but it's doable. Our temperament baseline may push one direction, but it doesn't control our lives. You may be prone to anger, but you're not destined to be violent.

On a related note, judging your temperament as good or bad is unproductive. Imagine owning a vast, empty field and framing it as *I hate this field. Why am I the one who owns this? It should have trees.* What does this frame accomplish? It doesn't change what you own. If you want trees, you need to plant them. The more time you waste lamenting instead of acting, the longer they'll take to grow.

In the same way, a particular temperament doesn't dictate someone's value. Being prone to frustration or anxiety is neither good nor bad, simply how one mind happens to operate. Baseline traits are outside your control. Focusing on changing them is only likely to cause frustration. You can, however, choose how to operate within your climate.

....

Working through frames, habits, and states constitutes all the heavy lifting needed to optimize happiness.

....

HOW DO FEATURES ARISE?

If you stumbled upon a new landscape, how would you explain the source of a particular feature? Without knowing the landscape's history, it would be hard to say. There are several ways a specific feature could have started. The only safe assumption is that either natural or human-made processes created it over time.

That may sound overly generic, but it is useful information. Whether hills or houses, some process created each landscape feature. If we control these underlying processes, we can make or remove features. We can build a ditch or drain a lake, even if their origins are obscure. By understanding the shaping processes, we can eventually reconfigure the landscape to our liking.

Similarly, each of our habits in thought, framing, and action were created by a process. By understanding these processes, we can control which mental features are strengthened or weakened. Much of our happiness is a result of these habits. In a later chapter, we'll explore how, with effort and intention, we can shift much of our default experience toward desirability.

HABIT OR TEMPERAMENT?

Highly ingrained habits are often confused with temperament, e.g., *I've had trouble speaking up my entire life. It's just part of who I am.* Each time we have a similar experience, the habit becomes more entrenched. The frames we choose often reinforce these even further. After many years of this cycle, it becomes hard to imagine acting differently. It may be challenging to see, but just because we're accustomed to something doesn't make it permanent. It takes significant effort and time, but even mountains are removable.

Most traits are malleable. How else can you explain massive shifts in personality? The shy high school student becomes an outgoing salesperson. The laidback associate becomes a tyrannical micromanager after being promoted. Changes are even faster and clearer following traumatic events. The rowdy, fearless soldier returns quiet and anxious. These transformations are relatively common and convincing evidence that many traits are malleable.

You might think: *Those are exceptions! Most people hardly change. I've known so-and-so for thirty years, and they're exactly the same as always.* Just because change can happen doesn't mean it necessarily will. Forests have grown for many years, mostly uninhibited until logging expeditions felled huge portions. Not everyone is exposed to circumstances that force change. It's still possible.

Most of us don't consciously choose to change habitual thoughts, frames, and reactions. Instead, we reinforce them with narratives like *I'm an introvert.* Our actions then support that belief, building evidence that it's true. With more examples, the belief grows more potent. It's a self-propelling cycle, pushing us toward a congruent identity. After ten, twenty, thirty years of this process, habits become significant and resilient features. For most, it seems daunting to unwind that much momentum.

In many cases, however, it is our only path to optimizing happiness. Dismantling notable features takes time: *I've been at it for months, I'll never be able to speak comfortably in front of others.* Don't get discouraged too quickly. Features built over many years can take years to dismantle, though the ratio is typically much better than one to one. Few aspects of life are purely temperament and out of our control. Before assuming a trait is a temperament, consider whether it might be a highly ingrained, but influenceable, habit instead.

LANDSCAPES AND MINDS EVOLVE CONSTANTLY

Another parallel between landscapes and minds is a continuous evolution. Your own mind may seem deceptively stable because you experience every sequential moment. Daily changes are so subtle we hardly perceive them. Yet, we almost certainly experience change over time.

Let's create a new perspective by expanding the timeline. Pick a point at least ten years ago, twenty or thirty if you can, and compare it to today. Who did you spend time with? What activities consumed most of your time? What were your biggest challenges and concerns? Even small habits may be different. What did you usually eat? When did you wake up? What was your favorite restaurant? It might be hard to remember exact details, but there have almost certainly been changes in your life, actions, or ideas since then.

This quick thought experiment can help illustrate. Imagine living in a small forest for ten years. You probably wouldn't notice much change. Maybe a few trees burned down or one of the trails washed out, but it would feel mostly the same. Now imagine leaving for ten years instead. Upon returning, you'd almost certainly notice the change. It wouldn't all be different, but it would be clear that processes are always at work, changing the forest's features slowly over time.

Our minds work similarly. Every experience slowly, subtly nudges us toward certain habits—whether or not we're conscious of them. Each day, we change slightly, every choice and environmental influence slowly shaping us along the way. This is inevitable. The only question is which parts of the process we want to exert influence over.

As you work to understand your mind and implement new processes, you may not notice an immediate change. Keep trying. Consistent effort creates results over time. The results build upon each other. Imagine the difference between ten years of consciously chosen, happiness-first adjustments and haphazardly hoping life comes together.

Curation of your mental processes isn't always easy, but it's more reliable than leaving it to chance.

A COMPLEX ECOSYSTEM OF INTERACTIONS

Landscape features don't exist in isolation; they're part of an ecosystem. All changes create side effects, no matter how small. Draining a lake impacts the surrounding plant life. Cutting down a single tree makes space for flowers or destroys a bird's home. Landscapes are large, interconnected planes where every action impacts the whole.

Our minds mirror this complexity. Changing habitual thoughts, frames, and responses doesn't happen in isolation. If we build discipline in our exercise routine that action branches into other realms. We may become more disciplined in other areas. Or we may feel more energized and clear-minded because of the exercise. Or our routine may be so intense that we're exhausted and unfocused for the rest of the day.

Each action creates a mental ripple. As you shape your mind, it's useful to consider all the potential impacts, not just the specific change. While no habit is inherently positive or negative, those that generally create positive momentum are the most useful. You want to optimize happiness across your entire mental ecosystem, not just isolated features.

INEVITABLE YARDWORK: UNPLEASANT EXPERIENCES

No matter how finely curated a landscape, there will be unpleasant events with corresponding work. Storms strike. Weeds grow. Windows break. Trees fall. Life always requires effort. We can't prevent that. We can, however, reduce the frequency of undesirable events and minimize corresponding difficulties. Some landscape features are universally unappealing. No one wants a field of weeds, worn paths, or an abandoned trash heap on their property. The difference is whether we're willing to put in the work to fix it. It's nearly impossible to stop weeds from growing, but we can renovate to the point that upkeep is minimal.

In the same way, life reliably produces undesirable states like loneliness, anxiety, jealousy, pain, etc. These states are inevitable, no matter how well we optimize because they communicate signals. They must be accepted as part of life. Instead of fighting them, we can determine how they're useful, act on that knowledge, and move forward.

The concept is easiest to digest when considering physical states. Imagine your body is incapable of physical pain. You decide to go for a run. Without physical feedback, you continue running for hours. Eventually, your legs start to wobble. You don't experience any sensation, so you keep running. At some point, they fail, causing irrevocable damage. You don't know why because you never felt any pain to indicate a problem.

A small percentage of people are actually born unable to feel physical pain. They don't learn from falling or burning themselves, and many experience fatal accidents at a young age. Without physical pain, the body can't signal when dangerous boundaries are crossed. Emotions work similarly, even though it may not feel this way intuitively. At the core, all emotional impulses serve some purpose. A spark of anger incites us to action. Loneliness signals a need for additional social interaction. Our frames can cloud the signal, but there is always a signal beneath our emotions.

Unfortunately, few of us are trained to process these signals. Instead of being aware and taking action, we often become lost in these painful emotions. We let them dictate our frames, which dictate subsequent states. Occasionally, we even frame neutral states in a way that manufactures unpleasant states. Take boredom, for example. Boredom is a low-grade signal that increased stimulation is currently more desirable. Nothing more, nothing less. It's common, however, to layer evaluations on boredom that create unpleasant states: *Nothing is exciting. I never feel engaged—what a waste of my time.*

These evaluations impact future evaluations: *I never do anything important or fun. What's wrong with me?* Before long, we've bolstered and transformed one signal of boredom into an entire day of sadness, frustration, and anxiety. Far removed from our initial state of low stimulation, we're still carrying forward and manufacturing unpleasant states.

While negative emotions are essential, you can create habits that marginalize the frequency and strength of these experiences. By changing your relationship with painful emotions, you can focus on the useful, underlying messages. In acting on those messages, the intensity dissipates, and you can move on faster. This is far more effective than the strategies typically employed.

One common but usually fruitless approach is trying to ignore or avoid unpleasant emotional states. This doesn't work because we also ignore or avoid the important signals these emotions communicate. Failing to address the root problem is like damming a river. The flow is blocked, which causes the signal strength and corresponding emotion to increase over time. Eventually, the intensity increases so much that we are forced to pay attention to the problem. By the time the dam bursts, the situation is always much more painful and difficult to manage. It's far more effective to identify, accept, and manage your emotions at the earliest point. Unpleasant emotions will always be a part of life, just like scraping your knee is always possible. You're aiming to build habits around cleaning and bandaging the cut instead of picking at it and distressing over the pain for hours. The work is necessary, but much of the pain is not.

UNDERSTANDING OTHERS' MINDSCAPES

While we'll primarily explore how mindscaping can optimize happiness, the concepts are also useful in understanding others. Accordingly, each major section includes a subsection viewing the topic through that lens. This both illuminates the framework from a second perspective and also produces useful insights for interacting with others.

For this section, the key concept is that each mindscape is unique, even if there are similarities between individuals. The details and nuances matter, and it pays to ask questions. We're often trying to understand a rainforest after living in a desert. Assumptions should be made sparingly, as even simple ones can lead to miscommunication and frustration.

Experiences are also unique to your mindscape. The same external experience can create different thoughts and feelings depending on states, frames, and focus. It's a light breeze in the desert compared to one in the tundra. The event is neither good nor bad, simply different relative to the environment. Navigating these nuances demands empathy, to the best of your abilities.

Here's an example: let's say your friend loves shopping. You, on the other hand, find shopping incredibly boring. You can't comprehend what's enjoyable about browsing clothes or luggage. For you, it's a waste of time, especially when you don't intend to buy anything. You might be inclined to think: *They enjoy something pointless.*

Let's examine this in terms of states and frames instead of our preferences. We now need to answer a specific question: How is that action producing desirable states or evaluations for them? Until we can answer that question, we cannot reasonably disparage the activity. No more, "I can't believe you enjoy x!" Instead, we must come to understand the process they're using to derive enjoyment.

Understanding before judging may seem like common sense, but it's frequently overlooked. Most believe their landscape's configuration is useful in determining how others should live: "You should go into medicine; it's what smart people do." This type of advice is well-intentioned but limited in its usefulness. Being a doctor may align with purpose and desirable outcomes in your mindscape, but what about theirs?

We must understand another's mindscape before we can understand what options might be desirable for them. Otherwise, we risk advising them that something like a jackhammer is the best tool in a desert. It may work great in your mindscape, but it won't ever work well in sand. Ask before assuming someone else's defaults and experiences closely match your own.

WITH THE THEORY OUT OF THE WAY . . .

Now we've covered the core concepts and can focus more on concrete material and practices. This is where effort starts counting. You might be tempted to read the strategy and skim the exercises instead of actually trying them. If you do this, you won't get the full experience nor give the framework a proper try. While you can still learn from the strategies, optimizing happiness requires actual effort.

While it may take time, I recommend completing all the exercises for the breadth of experience. Mindscaping is a cyclical process. You're likely to reuse effective tools many times. Exposure to multiple options lets you pick the best one for your situation, which will pay long-term dividends. Finally, be honest with yourself about the amount of effort you put in. If you expect results, you should also expect to work for them.

3

SURVEYING THE LAND – SELF-REFLECTION

Imagine walking through a landscape with no objectives, simply observing your surroundings. You notice a patch of weeds: *Seems like a great spot for a garden.* You're not busy, so why not start now? You pull up weeds, dig, and organize plots until sunset. It's looking good. You're excited to continue first thing in the morning.

You return home for some well-deserved rest. For someone who chose to wander and garden all day, it's not quite what you'd expect. "Home" is barely livable, unfurnished and in extreme disrepair. Windows are broken. The solitary door droops on its hinges. It's closer to a shed than a proper home. There's not even a bed, just a few somewhat soft items like books and plastic bottles piled on the floor. If anyone managed to fall asleep there, the quality would be abysmal. Who would prioritize a new garden with such an unlivable home?

Yet, many of our happiness journeys start similarly. We wander through our mindscape, haphazardly encountering features we want to improve, e.g., *I'd like to become a better public speaker.* We start work immediately and make progress yet are confused when life doesn't seem to improve. These are expected outcomes when we prioritize based on happenstance and fail to consider the greater context. Let's examine the example of motivations for public speaking more thoroughly. We need to ask:

→ Why do we want to learn public speaking?
→ How will this skill alter our states and/or evaluations?
→ Does it fit with other short- and long-term goals?
→ What is the opportunity cost of choosing to learn this instead of anything else?
→ What resources will we expend?

All these questions may seem like overkill, but they're important for prioritization and clarity. Time and effort are limited. To answer these questions, we must know what's most important in our current situation. We need clarity on the existing climate and features. Only then can we determine which changes will most increase happiness. Otherwise, assumptions may lead to gardening while our home collapses. Gaining this knowledge requires a meticulous self-survey process.

You might assume that you understand your own mind. After all, you spend all your time there, so you must be familiar with the nuances. But are you sure? Imagine a park you have visited many times. Do you know every plant species? How about the number of animals? Even after many visits, you're likely to have only a general familiarity with the place. You don't know every intimate detail because you didn't spend time intentionally encoding them in memory.

Our minds are similar. Most of us have a basic understanding, but few have spent substantive and concentrated effort becoming familiar with the nuances. Prevalent features are impactful, but unseen processes can be just as important. We may know how often it rains, but it's worth studying which plants grow best as well. Information critical to optimizing happiness is often locked away under surface-level understanding. That's why the self-survey is so important.

Essentially, the overall goal is building metacognition, which is awareness and comprehension of your own thoughts.

....

You must know your thoughts to understand your Mindscape and understand your Mindscape to optimize happiness.

....

PREPARE TO ACCEPT YOUR FINDINGS

There are several useful frames to consider before starting a self-survey. Most importantly, it may uncover unpleasant personal attributes. Naturally, we want to avoid painful truths, especially since negative frames often compound them. While reflection can be difficult, we must be grounded in reality to make future progress. Having a skewed view of our thoughts and actions makes it hard to choose effective tactics for optimizing happiness.

Self-judgment amplifies these challenging truths and should be avoided. Imagine it like a piece of property you absolutely must live on. Calling the place "good" or "bad" doesn't have any impact. You can only identify the property's characteristics and work from there. Building a home over a sinkhole requires fixing it first, whether you think the sinkhole is "good" or not. Wasting time on judgment and frustration only slows your progress.

The self-survey process also brings to light the relationship between self-acceptance and openness to development; they may seem like opposing ideas, but they can work in unison. We can accept and value ourselves while still seeing and undertaking opportunities to improve life. We can appreciate ourselves and our lives, yet want to optimize even further.

I'll use my relationship with physical health as a comparison. I could do more to be healthy. My posture isn't great, it doesn't take much running before I'm winded, and I'm not flexible enough to touch my toes. No matter how healthy I become, there will always be ways I can improve my health. When I evaluate physical health, however, I've trained myself to think of other attributes. For example,

I'm rarely in pain, I can run, and all my limbs work. I genuinely enjoy and appreciate those abilities. Seeing opportunities to improve doesn't diminish that frame.

I also recognize that to change a particular attribute, it must be in my control and something I choose to apply effort to. My height, for example, won't change, and I have no influence over it. I can think *I should be taller*, but it won't change anything. I'll only waste time choosing a frame that makes me feel bad. My cardiovascular health, on the other hand, is mostly within my control. My choices led me to my current position. Those are past choices, so they're beyond my control and not worth dwelling on. I can, however, influence future decisions. Choosing to focus on creating and implementing a plan will improve future states. Judgment and "shoulds" will not.

Judgment has no place in self-survey because it only ever makes us feel powerless—even for attributes we can influence. The more we focus on factors outside our control, the more likely we are to blame our entire lives on outside events. We start believing education, socioeconomic status, or genetics completely determine our lives.

....

Judgment can stop us from believing in the power of effort to produce change.

....

These are debilitating, time-sucking, self-fulfilling frames, and we will explore how to escape them later. For now, the point is accepting your current position and looking for further optimizations that are not inherently contradictory. It's all about how you choose to focus on and frame your experiences.

BE HONEST WITH YOURSELF

The second caveat is self-reflection must be entirely honest and realistic. It may be uncomfortable, but lying to yourself is worse. You can't make progress that way. Don't try to make yourself "look good." Don't justify past actions to escape current responsibility. Instead, remove labels and observe your mind as purely as possible. You may find it helps to act as though you're evaluating someone else, attaching your observations to another name.

There is no minimum bar in the self-survey. There's nothing to prove. Stretching the truth into the box of "good person" or "successful" may prevent you from seeing your mindscape for what it is. These positive labels may seem useful, but they're still judgments. They can also disguise serious happiness pitfalls. For example, *My job makes the world worse, but I'm still a good person because I donate 20 percent of my income to charity!* These justifications often restrict the very choices which will most optimize happiness.

It's like planning a pool when you know there's a layer of impenetrable rock an inch below the surface. You could dig out an inch, fill it with water, and call that a pool, but without digging deep and resolving the underlying issue, the feature will never be optimized.

....

Distorting reality undermines progress, sometimes stopping it completely.

....

Here's an example in daily life. Let's say you want to become a better conversationalist, so you decide to study storytelling. With practice, you successfully captivate increasingly larger audiences. Before long, you're regularly speaking to large crowds. Yet, private conversations are still heated and disconnected. It must be their fault. You can clearly communicate well, look at how many people listen to you! Right?

This situation may seem contrived, but it's precisely how we disguise flaws within the narrative of "being a good person" to avoid feeling uncomfortable: *I'm doing everything right. It's someone else making mistakes.* Instead of shifting blame, consider your influence on the situation. What is your role in this scenario? What could you change for the better? *I'm great at explaining my ideas, but maybe not at communicating respect for others' opinions. Once they get frustrated, I also get frustrated and escalate further.*

While objectivity is tricky, we need a clear, realistic perspective to see potential optimizations. This includes taking responsibility for everything we control and influence. This often forces us to push through the discomfort of being wrong, misguided, or confused. On the bright side, taking responsibility allows us to become stewards of our experiences instead of victims in a powerless, self-fulfilling narrative. This frame is far more reliable in producing desirable states.

INCREASE GRANULARITY OVER TIME

The mind produces far more information than we can possibly record and analyze. Each day brings a cascade of thoughts and actions. Luckily, we don't need all of it, only what's most important. Start with the most significant features and climate attributes, prioritizing what's most salient. After making high-level progress, you can repeat the process more granularly.

Mindscaping is cyclical, we increase our skills over time with each iteration.

Even with dedicated practice, we can't expect a perfect mindscape mapping, as they evolve constantly. In the same vein, tracking every event in every square inch of a landscape is equally infeasible. Fine-grained thoughts and habits shift rapidly. Instead of trying to comprehensively understand everything, we only need enough information to implement happiness-optimizing changes. We'll discuss implementation later, but don't get discouraged by the prospect of endless learning. Establish a productive baseline and keep moving forward.

UNDERSTANDING TEMPERAMENT AND CLIMATE

Understanding your mind requires familiarity with both your temperament and habits. We'll start with temperament, which parallels a landscape's climate. Temperament comes in the form of impulses and recurring tendencies that are rooted in biology. These attributes are resistant to change, even with significant effort. We can only optimize here by working with or around them.

Unfortunately, it's often hard to parse the distinction between nature and strongly ingrained habits: *Am I shy because I'm wired this way, or because it's all I've ever known? Have I built these habits over thirty years, or is it just who I am?* How can we know which factors are due to nature and which nurture? While arguing for binary positions is seductive, it's an oversimplification of reality. Most actions, thoughts, and behaviors aren't a result of either/or but a combination of both.

It's most useful to think of each trait on a spectrum. We can move across this range through effort, no position is entirely fixed. Our thoughts, actions, and environment interact with these baseline traits to produce our personality. Thinking about these specifically as number lines can help clarify the concept. Your baseline might be an 8/10 in risk-taking. Let's say that throughout your life, you take a few risks and face severely negative penalties. To avoid those unpleasant states in the future, you might consciously or unconsciously become a 6/10 in risk-taking. Experiences influenced your personality, pushing that trait below your original baseline.

Your range for risk-taking, however, might only be 2. That means, because of genetics, you'll never be below a 6 in risk-taking. However, while the impulse for risk-taking may never drop below a 6, your actions are still malleable. Our wiring only dictates impulses and baselines, not responses. Accordingly, we can continually push traits toward positions that produce desirable outcomes. We may hit diminishing returns after a certain point, but we can always make progress.

Still, some traits are definitely more fluid than others. Certain attributes are typically more change-resistant, with narrow ranges. These are the components we'll consider temperament. Here are a few traits which commonly have narrow ranges:

INTROVERSION/EXTROVERSION

Although introversion and extroversion are often used in common conversation to describe sociability, these traits more accurately map to how an individual's nervous system responds to stimulation. We recharge at either higher or lower levels of stimulation, depending on our genetics. Social occasions like parties include novelty, noise, and conversation, which are all high stimulation and suited to extroverts. This doesn't mean that introverts don't like socializing, they just recharge in lower stimulation environments.

As applied to mindscaping, it's essential to know which environments energize you, or you can end up feeling drained. This doesn't mean an introvert can't be a good salesperson, they just might need downtime at home afterward or fewer clients instead of a constant stream. An extrovert can be a good author, they just may need to socialize before and after writing a few chapters. The value is knowing how stimulation impacts us and planning accordingly.

RISK TOLERANCE: CONSCIENTIOUSNESS VS. IMPULSIVITY

Risk tolerance is another relatively stable trait. Some people are wired to act quickly. Others prefer extensive research. There are benefits and disadvantages to both. Slow, meticulous planning avoids impulsive decisions with poor long-term payoffs. Being too risk-averse, however, results in losing time-sensitive opportunities to indecision.

We can optimize our risk tolerance by finding frames and tools which nudge us toward good decisions. If we lean toward overanalyzing, we might timebox the decision by imposing a limit on research duration and a deadline for making the decision. If we're more instinctual, maybe we consult a few friends before deciding. Those are only a few potential options. Once you know the baseline, you can work with it toward an optimal solution.

EMOTIONAL REACTIVITY

Emotional reactivity is also relatively stable, though it refers to the intensity of emotional impulses, not reactions themselves. These impulses, like other experiences, exist on a continuum. Some people experience emotions much more intensely than others.

It might help to compare emotional reactivity to pain tolerance. Some people simply feel less pain because of their genetics, so they can handle moderately painful tasks more easily. Our ability to manage pain or emotional impulses is separate from how intense these feelings are. Yet, the threshold often determines how easily we become overwhelmed by intensity.

This means our difficulty in managing emotions is partially dependent on wiring. Reactivity can also differ per emotion. Controlling your temper might be easy, while for a friend, it requires significant investment into tools and habits. Reactions aren't inevitable, but stronger impulses are more challenging to moderate.

Returning to the landscape metaphor, I may process an experience as light rain, which you experience as a full downpour. This doesn't mean flooding is inevitable, but dealing with the increased volume of water requires stronger tools and more effort. Knowing the strength of your emotions and how to manage them effectively is critical to optimizing happiness.

SLEEP PREFERENCES

Are you a night owl or an early bird? While work schedules usually dictate sleep schedules, most of us shift toward our natural preferences when left unhindered. If you sleep in on the weekends, a later rhythm might be more natural for you (or you're sleep-deprived, which is also very common). While we can adapt patterns as necessary, our preferred sleep cycle tends to be stable in adulthood.

This trait is a prime example of how habits and discipline influence behavior. Even if our baseline is a late cycle, we can become accustomed to an earlier cycle after enough repetitions. If we stop attending to this habit, however, we gradually return to baseline. Changing our sleeping habits can be difficult, but it's a prime example of what effort and repetition make possible.

OPTIMIZING FOR TEMPERAMENT

These examples illustrate how we can approach our climate when optimizing. First, become familiar with your baseline. Your habits can take some time to differentiate. Once you know which traits are stable, consider how you can modify or work with them to optimize happiness. Impulses and baselines may be concrete, but reactions aren't. We have a lot of flexibility to modify our outcomes.

At this point, you may be wondering about tactical steps for optimizing. So far, we've only focused on temperament at a strategic level. Optimization requires action, but we'll cover that in a later chapter. In the meantime, there are a few simple examples that can help frame the concepts.

Say you're an introvert. If you know loud, busy environments are stressful, you can align your work environment accordingly. In an open office, you can book private rooms or negotiate part-time remote work. Without this knowledge, you may struggle to understand why work is so draining. Or maybe you're taking a finance course. No matter how hard you study, you can't remember the material. You start to feel like you'll never understand it. What if you know you learn best by reading, but you've only listened to lectures to study? With that knowledge, you could update how you study and improve your results.

These examples are both simple but common circumstances. Many of us don't understand our baseline traits very well, leading to suboptimal choices or problems we're unsure how to solve. This ultimately reduces pleasant states and limits productivity. The more we understand ourselves, the easier it becomes to make choices aligned with our baselines.

BASELINES DON'T DICTATE OUTCOMES

We've discussed how temperament influences outcomes, but there's more to unpack. Simply knowing this is not enough, we must also believe it. If we don't fully internalize the idea that effort can change outcomes, we are prone to self-sabotage. Without belief in change, change is unlikely.

When was the last time you heard personality used as an excuse for poor behavior?

—Sorry for being late. I can't help it; it's just who I am. I'm bad with time.

—You might think I'm being hard on you, but, hey, I'm just being honest. This is how I talk.

These types of beliefs provide an excuse to justify their actions, thus avoiding responsibility. This creates a pleasant emotional state now (*I am justified in these actions*) but has negative consequences for future purposeful states (*Why can't I create meaningful relationships?*).

While it may feel good in the moment, this is a net-negative strategy that limits our perception of control: *I'm bad with time.* There may be some truth here, like difficulty keeping time naturally. Yet, there are plenty of solutions.

You can easily set alarms or implement other tools as reminders. Individuals who assume baselines determine outcomes combine the two when really there's plenty of space for action.

It's also common to perceive our own traits inaccurately. We've all met people whose personal narrative doesn't match our experience of them:

"I'm really good with people. Everyone likes me!"

What? Everyone I know has a hard time working with you. I've overheard multiple instances of feedback about your abrasive communication style.

It may seem like I'm singling out annoying coworkers, but we're all susceptible to skewed self-perception. We craft narratives from a combination of our experiences, perceptions, and beliefs, but they're not guaranteed to be an accurate representation of facts. If a super-good-people-person isn't actually personable, maybe some "unchangeable" traits are actually malleable.

This isn't meant to cause a personality-based existential crisis, but to combat the belief that temperament forces behavior. Many of us carry this misguided belief because it's easier than changing ten, twenty, or thirty-plus years of habit formation. In reality, stable traits are more impulses and predispositions than predetermined behaviors. An inclination toward risk-taking isn't the same as actually taking risks. We can build new habits to intercept, modify, and direct these impulses. It may be difficult, but it's possible.

Consider the path of a hypothetical introvert. As a child, their introversion makes them uncomfortable around strangers (high stimulation without tools to moderate their natural impulses). As a way of coping with this discomfort, they withdraw and act shy. This strategy limits their social interaction. They develop the frame that interacting with others is uncomfortable. As they grow into adulthood, their shyness evolves into social anxiety.

This outcome wasn't predetermined. Particular experiences created a personal narrative of shyness. They framed feeling uncomfortable around others as an inevitable fact, creating reinforcing behaviors. As these behaviors became habitual, they became less likely to challenge the belief and explore more desirable options. Each subsequent experience reinforced the belief that socializing is uncomfortable. This led them to withdraw further and interact less, making each subsequent interaction more uncomfortable than the last.

Imagine the same individual with a few changes in their early life. As a child, they are uncomfortable around strangers and shy. Seeing this behavior, their parents teach them tools for managing discomfort. They also teach the frame that while some interactions are uncomfortable, creating connections is more important. While they are still likely to be drained by extensive social interaction, this individual is on a different path. Their experiences of socializing will compound differently. They will seek options for interacting effectively, making full-blown social anxiety a less likely outcome.

We can accept this responsibility for ourselves, acting as our own guides. This means consciously developing skills and habits to overcome happiness limiters. Most behaviors which produce unpleasant experiences aren't inherent weaknesses; they are ingrained habits using ineffective tools. With the right frames, effort, and experiences, we can shift traits across their ranges toward more desirable outcomes.

It may sound like I'm saying anyone can be anything if they try hard enough. *Stop telling people they can be anything! There are only so many Mozarts, Alexanders, and Einsteins.* I agree. I'm not saying you can be anything. Temperament traits *are* relevant to outcomes. Someone with a low baseline and a narrow range for aesthetics will never become the next Michelangelo. It's not that everything is possible; it's that attributes change across their range with repeated, dedicated action.

Let's say you're 5'3". Those base characteristics make playing in the NBA very unlikely. It's possible, but only barely. The rest of your skills would have to be phenomenal to overcome the height disadvantage (someone that height has played in the NBA before, by the way). Someone 6'8" has a much better baseline, but it's still possible at 5'3".

Now let's say you're 5'3" with an amputated arm and a blown-out knee joint. This baseline is at such a disadvantage playing in the NBA is effectively impossible. It's almost guaranteed other pursuits would optimize your time and happiness much more. I'm not preaching unfettered optimism but optimizing around realism.

Even with every disadvantage, however, you could vastly improve your skill. Your baseline might be low relative to professional athletes, but it doesn't prevent you from improving. You might improve tenfold from your baseline, but it wouldn't be enough for the specific goal of playing professional basketball. The important question is, would the time investment be a worthwhile trade-off? Would it optimize your states and evaluations? That's what matters.

You must be familiar with your temperament to know which investments are most worthwhile. Let's say you hardly interact with others. If you're happy with that, it may not be worth investing there. If it instead makes you miserable and disrupts other purposeful goals, it's probably worth the difficult effort to reconstruct those habits. It all depends on desires and impact on happiness.

TUNNELING: ASKING QUESTIONS FOR UNDERSTANDING

It's time we moved from conceptual strategy to practical tactics. We'll start with a general exploration tactic called "tunneling." This is a metacognition tool that can be used far beyond climate. Tunneling is mentioned throughout the book, and it's a tool we'll return to often. I recommend trying variants until you find one that works for you.

Tunneling is a fairly simple idea. It's the process of repeatedly asking *why* or other questions about our thoughts and experiences. This process unravels our beliefs, motivations, and frames, showing the roots of experiences. Along the way, we uncover steps in our thought process, highlighting potential points of influence, misperceptions, and distractions.

Here's an example, let's say I feel sick at work. I might ask:

—How is feeling sick impacting my life?

—It's an unpleasant state that's demanding lots of attention. My stomach hurts and I feel nauseous.

—Why am I feeling nauseous? How did this happen?

—I ate way too much junk food earlier.

That's pretty straightforward, but we can tunnel further to understand our actions and recognize decision points.

—Why did I eat so much junk food?

—Because it was enjoyable in the moment.

—Was it worth the trade-off?

—Not really.

—Why did I choose this behavior then?

—Because seeing sweets creates a strong impulses to eat them.

We've uncovered a useful fact. If seeing sweets triggers impulses to eat, we can act at that point: *How can I make sweets less visible, so I have fewer impulses?*

We'll explore change implementation later, but for now, focus on how tunneling uncovers where you have control. This process often requires practice and multiple iterations, but it surfaces points to alter decision chains. Acting at the easiest points in these chains can drastically improve outcomes. The idea is simple, but enacting the process effectively can be challenging.

Let's explore another example. This time you're reading a textbook, but not retaining much. You might ask:

—How can I better learn this material?

—A video with visuals would help a lot.

Here's a decision point, but let's go deeper.

—Why do I prefer information in video format?

—It's easier to pay attention.

—Why is it easier to pay attention?

—It's more entertaining, clearer, and I remember it better.

—Why is this the case?

—It's how I've always preferred to learn. I probably have better habits and tools for this style.

Decision points are immediately useful, but your general understanding also produces incremental benefits. At the end of a successful tunneling session, you should be able to reflect on a massive web of interconnected beliefs, experiences, and ideas. Each layer produces a deeper understanding of the system of your mind, how it impacts you and uncovers optimization options.

TUNNEL WITH NEUTRAL QUESTIONS

While tunneling, pay close attention to the quality of your questions. Many of us default to negatively framed questions like *Why am I a failure?* When the question implies an answer, the mind will work hard to answer accordingly. It will search for every failure it can possibly muster. If we want unbiased answers, questions must be neutral.

As a beginner, pay special attention to the emotional content of your questions. If emotions are anything other than neutral and curious, tunnel around the questions themselves.

- ➜ Why are negative frames being added?
- ➜ How often does this happen?
- ➜ How can the process be improved?

Shifting biased tunneling toward neutral tunneling might look like this:

—*Why am I a failure?*

—**That's negative.**

—*Why am I starting from a negative frame?*

—**Others call me that.**

—*Why am I allowing others' opinions to impact my self-worth?*

—**I value what other people say about me.**

—*Why do I care so much about what others think when it's out of my control?*

And so on . . .

Tunneling will help you to move beyond the initial emotion into questions that deepen self-understanding. It may seem like a detour from other problems, but emotional biases are often the most impactful frames we can work through. Locating the upstream cause of these frames allows us to treat the root instead of a symptom, cascading across many circumstances. (Note: Overly positive frames are similarly unhelpful, but to a lesser degree and are far less common.)

THEORY, EVIDENCE, EVALUATION

An alternative to tunneling is the theory, evidence, evaluation model, which outlines a similar but more rigid process. First, we craft a question or theory. Then, we look for factual, objective supporting evidence. We then evaluate the evidence and make a conclusion. With that conclusion, we create another theory, digging further into our thoughts. Essentially, it's a miniaturized version of the scientific process.

Here's what the process looks like, starting with an event, such as a rejection after a job interview with no feedback. Imagine having the thought *I'll never get a job I like.* While this is framed with negative emotion, we'll use it as our starting point.

Theory: *I'll never get a job I like.*
Evidence: *I've had the same job for three years and was rejected during one job interview.*
Evaluation: *My evidence is only one attempt. A huge range of factors could have resulted in the rejection. It may not be directly because of my skills.*

After comparing our theory against objective evidence, there's not much support. A sample size of one isn't very reliable. Here, the process helps move us away from binary assumptions toward positive, productive, and creative thoughts. For example, something like this:

Theory: *Applying to more jobs might help me find something better.*

Evidence: *Most people apply to multiple jobs before getting an offer.*

Evaluation: *I should send more applications and wait for the results.*

Or

Theory: *There must be a way to get a job I'll like more.*

Evidence: *Other individuals have jobs like the one I want.*

Evaluation: *I can ask someone with my dream job how they got there. I can model my path after their answer.*

You can continue this process indefinitely, feeding your evaluations into new theories. Of course, the examples are streamlined. Thinking at this level of objectivity is challenging, especially during emotionally challenging times. It takes practice to consistently generate realistic theories, evidence, and evaluations. Writing out your thoughts can ease the process—this forces clarity throughout the thought chain.

While this process is more formal, it also provides clear steps for evaluating thoughts. It's a soft steppingstone into personal reflection. This can break negative spirals, as well as provide productive next steps, and it becomes faster and more natural with practice.

Moving forward, we'll refer to both variants as tunneling. Your preferred flavor isn't important, just that you have a tool handy for analyzing thought processes. Analyzing thoughts effectively is core to this framework and essential for optimizing habits. This skill takes time to develop, so don't be alarmed if it's difficult at first.

TOOLS FOR UNDERSTANDING YOUR CLIMATE

Tunneling is a general-purpose tool, but most of the tactics in this book are relevant to a particular realm. These tactics are generally effective, but that doesn't mean they're guaranteed to work for everyone. I recommend trying them all, so you can see which ones fit you best. Then you can mix and match based on what has produced the best results. In this chapter, our focus is on self-reflection tools for developing metacognition.

ISOLATED SELF-REFLECTION

The first tactic for doing a self-survey is isolated self-reflection. We're always in our mindscape, yet we're distracted most of the time. We're buying groceries, having a conversation, or navigating traffic, not exploring our thoughts. It's like flying over a landscape with the windows closed. We're technically in the landscape but not paying attention to it. We need to spend time on the ground, examining details to learn about it. Isolated self-reflection can produce this effect.

Isolated self-reflection doesn't mean becoming a hermit and refusing contact for six months. It simply means breaking free from the usual flow of life to think clearly without distraction. In theory, this is simple. In practice, not so much. Our minds are accustomed to constant stimulation. Sitting alone with our thoughts for even a few minutes can be a lot more challenging than it sounds.

Implementing this tactic requires planning time, specifically for contemplating, and eliminating all other inputs. That means disconnecting from phones, computers, people, and all other potential distractions. It often requires doing lower-stimulation activities, like hiking, finding an empty coffee shop/bookstore, or driving on an open highway. With some effort, you can escape external stimulation and be alone with your thoughts.

Isolated reflection sessions don't have to be lengthy, formal, or serious to be useful. All it takes is blocking out some time with the intention of self-understanding. You can set a specific topic, like health, or just see what thoughts arise. Priorities will tend to bubble to the surface. From there, you can tunnel through those thoughts for deeper insights.

Isolation and intention alone are often sufficient to create a productive session. If you're having trouble, however, try combining isolation with some of the following, more structured tools. They'll provide clearer steps while minimizing distractions, which will improve the quality of your focus and insights.

HISTORICAL SELF-ANALYSIS

Our next self-survey tactic is a historical analysis of thoughts and actions. This practice is essentially writing down important events and repeated patterns. This exercise may seem trivial—*I know about my life, I lived through it*—but the process of writing down events and looking for patterns is much more intentional. It's the difference between watching a movie and writing an analysis of its thematic elements.

Start by finding somewhere you can write undisturbed for at least ten minutes. Then write down every important event, goal, or choice you can recall, starting from childhood. Memory is imperfect, so there are likely to be large gaps. Perfection isn't the goal; just do your best to formalize what has been important throughout your life. Home in on emotionally salient events, as those are often important and detail-rich.

I've included an off-the-cuff example of what this might look like. It's written in paragraphs, but you can use bullet points, a word web, or any other format. Tweak the style to fit your preferences; you're not tied to what I've done here.

My first thought is that I've always liked games. I like the challenge and the feeling of winning. I guess it's because I'm competitive. I remember being two years old and wanting to win. I'd get frustrated not when I lost, but when they weren't challenging. I've always played sports, too, often in competitive leagues. I always felt motivated to push my limits to win. I can easily tap into a competitive spirit and produce work. Maybe this is useful information for staying motivated in other realms as well.

Continue like this until you run out of ideas, taking breaks, and organizing themes as needed. This may seem daunting, messy, and time-consuming, but it produces a large volume of reflection material. Even a few paragraphs contain substantial information to consider. If you think there's a pattern, you can always tunnel deeper. Before long, the subtle border between strong habits and temperament impulses will become clearer.

I've crafted a few primer questions in case you get stuck. These aren't the only viable topics, just a few that might help you start. Exploration beyond these questions is also highly recommended.

- What activities have you always enjoyed? Why?
- Which activities have you always disliked? Why?
- What themes have you repeatedly seen throughout your life?
- What are your biggest life milestones and accomplishments?
- What are the biggest decisions you've made? Do you regret these choices or enjoy them?
- Which traits have most influenced your important decisions?
- What impulses are consistent throughout your life?
- What are you most proud of? Least proud of?

TREAT YOURSELF LIKE A NEW FRIEND

While most advocate against talking to ourselves, it's actually a useful reflection tool (just, maybe not in public). We all carry baggage, so getting an objective view of ourselves can be hard. Framing our self-survey under the guise of interviewing someone else often creates mental space for genuine, neutral exploration. This won't eliminate all biases, but it helps shift perspective externally.

Talking to yourself may seem odd, but most of us do some variant of it regularly: *What do I want for lunch? Why do I feel so lazy today? Why do I like this person?* In essence, we're using common thought sequences more intentionally by tunneling for patterns and opportunities. Instead of occasionally asking ourselves random questions, we do it with the intention of understanding traits.

To start this exercise, imagine you're interviewing someone. Write down a list of questions you'd use to get to know them better. Unlike a new acquaintance, don't be afraid to ask meaningful and highly personal questions. Then, go through and answer each question yourself, tunneling along the way. Here are a few examples:

- → How do you most enjoy spending time?
- → How would you describe your personality?
- → What are your most important values?
- → How did you choose your line of work or area of study?
- → What are you working toward right now?
- → What are you passionate about?

- ➔ What do you want to accomplish?
- ➔ What do you care about most in the world?
- ➔ If money weren't an issue, what would you most want to do?
- ➔ What are you most afraid of?
- ➔ What do you think you're best at?

Starting externally helps surface powerful questions you may not have considered otherwise. The difficulty of these questions depends on how much you've thought about them previously. If your initial answers feel routine, tunnel further into them for greater understanding. Oh, and maybe go somewhere private to avoid the social stigma of talking to yourself.

PERSONALITY TESTS

Personality tests are another useful self-survey tool. On the surface, they require little work; answer a few questions and review the results. With this simplicity come caveats. Primarily, the validity of most, if not all, personality tests is contested. You might get consistent results if you're lucky, but do they map to immutable personality traits? The answer is complicated and test-dependent. Luckily, we can avoid the debate entirely. Instead, we'll discuss how personality tests can be a useful reflection tool, regardless of accuracy.

Instead of accepting personality tests at face value, we can use the questions about behavior and preferences to slow down and reflect. Answers that feel particularly complex are good opportunities to tunnel.

You can also use the results to spark reflection. Before taking any conclusions too much to heart, be skeptical of the test quality. For example, binary results are a red flag, because almost all traits exist on a range. You're either angry or sad. Energetic or lethargic. Mean or nice. While convenient labels, life rarely fits into such clean boxes. Personality is no exception.

So instead of focusing on accuracy, compare your results against your experience. What's correct? What misses the mark? How do you know? If this were true, what would it say about you? If this was false, what would that mean for you? As mentioned in tunneling, be especially wary of framing effects. Your mind will find what you ask it to, so priming in a certain direction is likely to yield results. Use these tests for reflection, not as a guide for what your life is destined to be like.

This style of analysis allows even the most scientifically dubious tests, like what fruit you are, to produce useful contemplations. If you want to take a scientifically backed test, however, The Big Five has the most scientific credibility right now (MTBI is popular but supporting science is marginal at best). Even the Big Five has been subject to a wide range of criticism, though. Don't accept the results of any test blindly.

ASK OTHERS

There's only so much reflection we can do on our own. Adding outside perspectives increases the quality and accuracy of our evaluations. Accordingly, asking close connections about our traits improves the accuracy of our self-survey. Each individual produces a unique account of how they view us. By combining data from multiple sources, you can unlock insights that would otherwise be impossible.

Asking others about your personality requires some preparation. First, decide which individuals you trust to be honest. When completing a self-survey, biased information is unhelpful. Second, it helps to craft a list of questions. By providing context and direction, you're more likely to get specific, focused, and useful answers.

Both open-ended and specific questions work, depending on your goals. Open-ended questions are ideal for gathering general information. For example: "What do you think my strengths are?" Or "How would you describe me?" Open questions force the individual to construct the entire answer themselves. This creates more raw information, but these types of questions are harder to answer. Unfocused questions are also more likely to result in answers that wander off-topic.

Specific questions are the tools of choice when we have theories about ourselves. For example, "I'm trying to improve my communication skills, how often have you noticed me interrupting?" This question presents one specific idea, allowing them to verify or contest your conclusion.

Ask for examples if you can. Others' perceptions increase the evidence we can draw on, making our self-image more accurate.

While useful, all opinions should be digested slowly and carefully. Just as self-surveys have gaps, some individuals produce inaccurate or unhelpful information. Don't take everything at face value. Instead, look for trends. If one person considers you rude, but fifteen think you're polite, you're probably generally polite. Increasing feedback volume can help determine what's likely to be true.

PREPARING FOR HONEST FEEDBACK

Giving and receiving feedback can be difficult, so be clear that you are able to digest comments without becoming upset or defensive. The most straightforward way to accomplish this is by explaining you want honesty for realistic insights about yourself. The more earnest you are, the more likely you'll get thoughtful answers.

This can be a challenging process. You should prepare to accept negative feedback before asking anyone for their opinion. Negative comments can cause a surge of emotions. In some instances, it may feel like they're intentionally attacking you. Dismantle this frame. It's more likely they don't know how to communicate positive intentions softly. You also may feel the need to defend yourself. Don't argue. You must be willing to digest feedback, even if you disagree.

Look for positive intent in what's said to you. For example, if someone says, "You're getting fat," the positive intent is "I'm concerned for your health." Their frame and word choice are terribly miscalculated, but they ultimately have good intentions. This can be quite challenging since these statements often elicit emotions. If you start feeling overwhelmed, give yourself space. Take a break. There's no reason to force the conversation. Revisit the ideas, looking for positive intent, when you feel more relaxed.

Ideally, frame feedback within pure curiosity. In this mindset, you can sidestep emotional evaluation, focusing on clarity and follow-up questions. As with other reflection techniques, these questions should be neutral. For example, if they say, "You're just not attractive," you might ask: "How do you define attractive?" But not, "Why are you trying to make me feel bad?"

This is productive, but by no means natural. We're wired to worry about how others perceive us. If evaluations of you seem negative, emotions often surge to signal that action is required. We must learn to cope with these feelings if we want to use feedback effectively. This takes time and practice. Don't feel obligated to take it all on at once, you can always get more feedback later.

PROCESSING FEEDBACK

We can further reduce the emotional tax of feedback by categorizing it based on usefulness. The model we'll use details three categories: empty, vague, and specific. While this model is primarily used to depersonalize negative feedback, the categories apply to positive and neutral feedback as well. Our goal is to use feedback to determine what behavior changes we can make for better outcomes.

Empty feedback contains no concrete or useful information. For example, "You're so awesome!" Or "You suck at this." While these statements have an emotional quality, there's no underlying content. You can't answer, "What can I learn from this?" Or "What should I do based on this feedback?" There's no information about potential behavior changes to improve outcomes. If you receive empty feedback, either ask for a specific example or ignore it entirely.

Vague feedback is slightly better as it contains ideas, but they lack clear action steps or instances. For example, "You just aren't qualified," or "People seem to like working with you." Vague feedback provides a realm of behaviors without narrowing down anything specific. In these instances, suggest specific behaviors or ask follow-up questions digging for specifics. For example, "When you say people like working with me, what do you think they enjoy? That I'm reliable? That I listen?" In the best case, this will convert vague feedback into detailed feedback. In the worst case, you'll have to determine potential changes yourself based on the realm of behaviors.

Detailed feedback has both a useful idea and specific actions, either previously taken or possible in the future. For example, "You need more tools to manage your temper. Last week you were upset because it took two tries to get the deadbolt undone. You were short with everyone for an entire hour afterward. Maybe you should try deep breathing when you feel these emotions building, so they don't spill out into your relationships." In this example, we get the idea, details of an incident, and ideas for future action. The level of detail makes tunneling deeper easy.

Why was I so upset about the deadbolt? Was I frustrated before this? Was I tired? Why did I stay upset for so long? How can I manage this better in the future? Detailed feedback provides enough information to spark useful questions. We should strive to provide this quality of feedback to others and use follow-up questions to elicit it when soliciting feedback for ourselves.

Slotting feedback into this model helps depersonalize it and maintain objectivity. Typically, the most emotionally charged feedback is the least useful. By pushing feedback toward details instead of emotions, we can focus on productive change instead of managing emotions. This framework makes it easier to identify what's not useful and discard it more quickly. In essence, feedback loops become faster, less stressful, and more productive, as they're intended to be.

UNDERSTANDING HABITS: ENVIRONMENT FEATURES

We're now shifting from climate-survey tools into feature-survey tools. For a quick recap, habits are equivalent to features in a landscape. These features are shaped by each action and experience, whether by chance or intention. The larger a feature is, the more likely it is to be chosen automatically instead of consciously. Accordingly, it can be hard to distinguish established features from climate attributes.

Before we can discuss habit change, first we need to identify which features exist and at what magnitude. Dismantling a mountain requires a different strategy than moving pebbles. We need to determine how much water we already have before creating a lake. In the same way, we must be familiar with current behaviors before we can accurately scope a particular project. Without this knowledge, our plan is likely to be derailed by unexpected roadblocks along the way.

Imagine shoveling several loads of dirt onto the same spot every day. After a few weeks, the mound would be too heavy to remove in a day, even if you worked nonstop. After a year, it would take substantial effort to move, even with stronger tools. After a decade, it would take significant time using heavy machinery to dismantle your small mountain. Imagine reversing it with only a shovel.

No matter how large, however, it could eventually be dismantled and returned to baseline. It just requires removing a few shovelfuls of dirt every day instead of adding them. You could do it even faster if you found other, more powerful tools. It would take time and effort either way, but you could absolutely remove the entire dirt pile. Habits are similar in many ways.

As we survey habits, we'll find some more entrenched than others. There will be mounds, hills, and mountains. Some may be so large you'll have trouble conceptualizing living differently, even though it's possible. Remember, all features are subject to the influence of intentional, repeated action. Some projects may be massive undertakings, but we can choose the mounds of dirt we want to move.

You may notice tactics for surveying habits overlap somewhat with temperament. As previously mentioned, they can be difficult to disentangle. Temperament often feeds habits, and many habits are strong enough to seem like a personality trait.

....

Don't worry about perfectly categorizing each type of behavior. Focus on the exercises and learning more about yourself. Distinguishing your habits will become easier as you gain experience.

....

TRACK DAILY ACTIONS

We can't rely on memory for information about behavior because more happens in a single day than can be remembered and facts blend together over time. Tracking daily actions provides far more reliable data. After tracking for a while, we can easily answer the questions: *How do we spend time each day?* And *What decisions are made?*

Tracking may sound overwhelming, but recording every minute of every day isn't necessary. You can spend just a few minutes recording what stood out throughout the day. If that turns out to be insufficient, granularity can always be increased later.

The hardest part is remembering to record the data. An easy way to start is setting two timers, spaced across the day. When the timer goes off, write down the day's salient events. It might look something like this:

Mid-Day:

Woke up at 8:15, late (also went to bed late).

Road rage during my commute.

Distracted and unfocused in the office.

Frustrated with coworkers being too loud.

Had lunch with a friend, very enjoyable.

Night:

Stuck in traffic, home at 7:30 pm.

Skipped workout because of traffic.

Watched episode of a TV show.

Read for 10 minutes.

Bed at midnight.

Even with such a small investment, patterns quickly emerge. Two weeks' worth should be plenty for creating a good sample to dig through for patterns.

- ➜ What themes are recurring—default and important?
- ➜ What impact do these patterns have?
- ➜ What changes could you make to improve outcomes?

For example, maybe you notice you are regularly frustrated with your coworkers. That's a sign to tunnel further. Why are you getting frustrated? How can you optimize the situation? Do you need a different job? A different type of work? A different environment? Better tools to handle frustration? Tools to build relationships?

Tunneling through these patterns allows you to uncover underlying causes and action steps. If you get frustrated because your coworkers are too loud, many solutions become clear. Get headphones or earplugs. Work elsewhere part of the time.

....

By analyzing reliable data, our optimization decisions become more reliable as well.

....

RECOGNIZE AND TRACK TRIGGERS

Another even easier way to track actions is to look for triggers. Triggers, in this context, means impulses or strong emotions following a particular activity. Often, these chains of behavior happen unconsciously. When we look at them more closely, we see the relationship between certain events and subsequent actions. With the whole chain in mind, we can make wise decisions about which point in the chain we have the most influence over and optimize accordingly.

Events often become paired with specific impulses. For example, you might always have the impulse to eat cookies after coming home from a long day. Or you might always feel the urge to make conversation when you see someone looking uncomfortable. Maybe you have the urge to go for a run whenever you wake up early. These default triggers guide many of our decisions, for better or worse.

Those are benign examples, but powerful, potentially destructive triggers also exist. For example, seeing alcohol may create the impulse to consume alcohol, regardless of how much you've already had. Or maybe feeling unhappy creates the impulse to spend money, regardless of your bank balance. Repeatedly following these impulses can significantly decrease our quality of life.

That's why tracking triggers is so useful, especially when we tunnel to understand the entire chain. To try this tactic, set out time each day to write down paired activities. Expand on them as much as possible. The more tightly you can tie events to subsequent actions, the more useful the information will be. It's similar to daily tracking, but much more focused on cause and effect instead of raw reporting. There's no right way to do this, but here's an example:

Monday:

Stressed from work, felt like napping all day even though I slept well last night.

Wednesday:

Got my paycheck, which made me think of retirement. Thinking about retirement made me feel anxious for the rest of the day.

Saw coworkers running at lunch today. I went to the gym after work.

Thursday:

Noticed someone jogging on my drive home, decided to go to the gym instead.

Saturday:

Stressful doctor's appointment. Wanted to sleep afterward.

Notice the focus on connections between events and subsequent actions and/or feelings. These can validate other self-survey assumptions, such as *I always want to sleep when I'm stressed,* with actual evidence. Tunneling to expand the analysis can also lead to unanticipated root causes, which are often much easier to influence.

As with other tactics, noticing triggers in the moment can be difficult at first. It takes time to build a habit around remembering to look for pairings. Again, alarms or highly visible notes (bathroom mirror, steering wheel, etc.) are useful reminders. Even so, it's normal to miss triggers or have trouble connecting events to behaviors in the beginning. Don't worry. Your mind will become more attuned to recognizing chains over time.

WHERE DO THOUGHTS COME FROM?

Before discussing the next tactic, we need to take a slight detour through the origin of thoughts. A common assumption is that we (our consciousness) creates and controls all our thoughts. This doesn't quite hold up under scrutiny. Some thoughts are intrusive, arriving with no conscious input. They enter our conscious mind but aren't necessarily our thoughts in the sense that we consciously created them.

Imagine watching a dance show when suddenly the thought, *I should start a bakery*, crosses your mind. Where did that thought come from? If you think you created it, how did you do it? It wasn't the conclusion of a sequence of coherent thoughts. It's not the direct result of a stimulus you saw. It simply popped into your mind, uninvited. Perhaps it's a venture you've thought about before, but nothing consciously available spawned that exact thought at that exact moment.

An initial thought may spur further contemplation. Subsequent thoughts may be a direct result of conscious activity, but we still can't explain the original thought as a product of consciousness. Some other mental process created it, then presented it to your consciousness. This may sound strange and unintuitive, but realizing we don't author all our thoughts allows us to create space from unpleasant ones. Many thoughts are not from "us" or our consciousness, but other parts of the mind. The book *Thinking Fast and Slow* is a great deep dive into this topic.

Here's another example. Most of us will have experienced some variant of a strange, violent, or inappropriate thought, image, or impulse. *I should crash my car into a building. I want to push that person. I want to force myself to throw up for no reason.* While they may cause alarm, we almost never act on these thoughts. Conscious processes take control and dissipate the impulse. At a certain level of extremity, dissociating from a thought becomes easier.

Extreme examples, however, are certainly not the only case of outside thoughts appearing in our consciousness. For this reason, taking ownership of and identifying with all our thoughts can cause problems. The concept is important enough that I'll illustrate with another, more personal example.

My mind occasionally creates thoughts like *I hate my life,* even during activities I enjoy. When I took ownership of these thoughts and accepted them as "me," these impulses overwrote other states. *Hmm. I'm enjoying this movie, but I just thought about how much I hate life. That must be right. What's wrong with me? Why can't I be happy even during enjoyable activities?* Even during positive states, identifying with intrusive thoughts lead to negative evaluations. I didn't know there was a space between thoughts arising and my conscious experience.

While I now experience less of these intrusive thoughts, they still happen occasionally. I'm no longer distressed or disturbed when something frightful like, *I want to die*, randomly pops into my mind. I know I don't have to identify with it. I recognize I never chose to have that thought. The reasons my mind created the thought may not be known, but ultimately I choose how to evaluate it.

It's worth attempting to tunnel into the roots of unpleasant intrusive thoughts. This may uncover important insights for happiness-optimizing projects. For example, wanting to crash might be a sign of depression. It's also possible we find nothing and can accept the intrusive thoughts as a side-effect of the way our mind works. Maybe tunneling through wanting to throw up has no discernable origin or purpose. We can simply discard orphan thoughts if they're not useful, but checking for other signals is worthwhile.

Repeated, powerfully intrusive thoughts can signal a problem, and if your intrusive thoughts are high intensity or regularly cause distress, I recommend seeking professional help. It's tough enough to parse common intrusive thoughts. When they're more frequent and more powerful, there's almost definitely a relevant root cause, and an expert should be enlisted to help.

It can be hard to digest the idea that we're separate from our thoughts. Few of us have been exposed to this frame, and for many, it's a full paradigm shift. Adopting this frame, however, is incredibly important in understanding and optimizing our minds. If this concept is confusing, I strongly recommend revisiting this section as well as other resources on the mechanics of thought. Clarity here will go a long way in creating optimized frames.

OBSERVE YOUR THOUGHTS AS THEY ARISE

Understanding how thoughts arise opens new tactics for doing a self-survey. We generally experience thoughts in a constant stream, unaware of the transitions between them. Few of these thoughts are examined and explored more deeply. Intentionally increasing the regularity of these examinations illuminates each step of the process. That's our aim in observing thoughts as they arise. This is similar to tunneling; however, here we're focused on thoughts that come into our consciousness but were generated elsewhere in our minds.

This is one of the most challenging exercises in this book. We're used to living in and as our thoughts. Ceasing to identify with them is difficult enough, let alone creating space to analyze them. As an initial step, try this short exercise. Close your eyes and observe your thoughts. Don't try to guide or change the thoughts, simply let them come. It's like watching a movie, where the content is whatever comes to mind. Try this for a minute or two before moving on.

If you did the exercise, there's a good chance your thoughts first focused on content in this section. *OK, my eyes are closed. I'm sitting here thinking. I'm not really sure what the point of this is. I'm thinking about thinking. OK, still here. Waiting for . . . what? What is the point of this?* And so on.

Given long enough, however, a thought from an entirely different thread will arise. *I wonder if it has been a minute yet. I'm excited to wear the new shirt I bought today.* Wait. What? Where did that thought come from? It just as easily could have been *I wonder what to make for dinner* or *I forgot to wash my car last week.* Where did that thought come from? Try the exercise one more time with this in mind.

When we regularly practice observing our thoughts, we start to feel space between when they arise and our conscious evaluation of them. Feeling this space provides significant control over our decisions. We can inject extra thoughts between an impulse and our reaction. For example, say your mind often produces negative self-talk about your intelligence. You might be driving and suddenly think *I'm stupid,* completely unprompted. We can recognize the thought separate from our identity and tunnel through it. *Is that a belief I actually hold about myself? How often does it occur? How useful is this? Where did this come from?*

Perhaps the first question is enough to break the chain. You don't actually believe you're stupid. Your focus can then shift to future actions for dismantling similar thoughts. *When I think I'm stupid, I won't feed that thought. Instead, I'll force myself to recall a time when I felt smart. Or when I catch myself thinking I'm stupid, I'll view the thought with curiosity then immediately stop focusing on it. I'll find something more useful to focus on instead.*

This immediately disempowers the negative intrusive thoughts before they replicate. In the long term, repeated, positive frames reshape our mind's background chatter. Talking to ourselves this way may seem silly, but we're training our minds to produce more productive thoughts. We won't completely eliminate intrusive thoughts, but we can better manage them and push for a more positive default. It's certainly better than the alternative of identifying with and feeding self-sabotaging thought loops.

Two common methods for observing thoughts are spontaneous journaling and meditation. Spontaneous journaling means writing thoughts with no hesitation. You write every thought, unfiltered. The writings don't have to be fully formed sentences or even coherent ideas. You simply write what comes to mind. It might look like this:

I'm sitting here. I'm not sure I like the pace of this song. I think I'll skip it. There's an itch on my leg. The mirror above me seems positioned in a strange place. I wonder when my partner will be home from work.

This may seem random, but it provides tangible data to analyze thought sequences. It also highlights how erratically thoughts arise, based on whatever happens to catch your attention. After writing a series of thoughts, you can then practice exploring the source of each one.

- ➤ I'm sitting here (perception of physical state).
- ➤ I'm not sure I like the pace of this song (auditory state evaluation).
- ➤ I think I'll skip it (action based on an evaluation).
- ➤ My leg is itchy (physical state).
- ➤ The mirror above me seems positioned in a strange place (visual state evaluation).
- ➤ I wonder when my partner will be home from work (unprompted thought).

This technique is especially kind when you're starting out because it provides unbounded time to analyze each thought. This avoids juggling between experiencing and exploring thoughts. Instead, you can record the thoughts and then explore them later at your own pace. The downside of spontaneous journaling is that translating thoughts into writing is slow. It's unlikely to capture your full conscious experience. Our thoughts tend to move much faster than our hands. Meditation provides a far richer experience, observing thoughts as they're populated.

Before going further, I'll clarify what's meant by meditation here, as the word often creates assumptions. There is a vast range of meditative styles. We won't cover them in this book (I don't even know them all), but many people find some form useful. The topic is worth exploring beyond this book. In this context, however, meditation simply means spending time observing your thoughts as they arise.

Allowing thoughts to flow freely while also observing them is challenging. Attention must cycle between thought and observation. Expect your attention to be consumed by thought many times per session, then brought back to observation. If you've never tried formal meditation or anything similar, guided practices are a good place to start. Otherwise, you can try this exercise by simply setting a timer, finding a place with no distractions, and observing thoughts as they arise.

SURVEYING OTHERS IS EVEN HARDER

Navigating the many layers of our mindscape is already difficult. Now imagine surveying it from another planet, in the dark, with limited time and tools. This is precisely how much more difficult it is to understand other mindscapes. You may see prevalent features, but there's significantly more information buried under the surface. We can become familiar with how others typically think, but we can never fully grasp their experience.

That doesn't mean working at relationships is futile. On the contrary, it's one of the most purposeful activities in which we can engage. Instead, the point is that it's unwise to predict others' thoughts and experiences, even if you know them well. Their mindscape likely differs from your assumptions. Not all tundras have frozen lakes. A desert doesn't necessitate dunes.

This also means not jumping to conclusions based on a limited sample of actions. If we don't have the full picture of our closest relationships, we're definitely missing information in interactions with strangers. If someone is rude, maybe they're just having a bad day. Or maybe they're bad at communicating, but genuinely have good intentions. Our perspective is only the surface layer, which often isn't enough for fully informed empathy.

We choose the frame for resolving ambiguous scenarios. Giving others the benefit of the doubt while staying open to new information feels better. Defaulting to good intentions creates desirable frames during uncertainty. Staying open to new information protects us from malicious intent while allowing increased empathy. If we don't know the whole story, we might as well pick the nicest version which fits our current knowledge.

HOW SELF-AWARE ARE OTHERS?

Most people live without questioning actions or ingrained habits too deeply. They haven't been exposed to metacognitive tools or compelling steps for how to change results. Many also believe temperament is fixed and that it predetermines outcomes. In that mindset, it's hard to determine which efforts actually improve life. If you think outcomes are stable, it makes sense to quit when results don't come quickly.

Regardless of the underlying reasons, the outcome is similar: a life based on defaults instead of intention. The execution of routines without analysis of how behaviors, thoughts, temperaments, and habits impact happiness. This rarely leads to the best outcomes. There's no judgment here; you must be aware of tools to consider using them. Most people simply haven't seen a comprehensive toolset for optimizing happiness.

Here's an example. Let's say you need to dig a hole. The only tool you've ever used is a hand shovel. You don't know larger shovels exist, and the idea of machinery like an auger is completely beyond your imagination. With that knowledge, you'll dig the hole with a hand shovel, never realizing better solutions exist. Even if the results are subpar, you're not aware of alternative tools.

Framing others' actions this way makes frustrating situations more digestible. Imagine a friend who is defensive toward criticism, even if it's constructive. They may not be aware of tools for deconstructing criticism to find what's valuable. They may also habitually add negative frames to neutral feedback. They may not realize this event chain can be modified. How can we expect them to reach for an auger when they only know shovels exist?

Speaking of which, let's return to our digging example. Let's say, one day, you actually encounter an augur. It's completely new and foreign. The vast majority of us would have thoughts like *What is this thing? I know hand shovels work, is this worth trying? Is it better? Can I even learn this after so many years?* And so on.

Even with exposure, others may not have the knowledge and beliefs to integrate new tools effectively. Most people have seen wildly inconsistent results from their effort, so it's unsurprising they often resist change. They don't want to waste time and energy if they don't see the path to success. The status quo is far easier to maintain, especially if it's already somewhat effective.

These frames can make potentially frustrating interactions more digestible. Before becoming upset or passing judgment, consider their habits and history. What tools have they been exposed to? Are they aware of alternatives? Are they aware of the consequences of their actions? Why do they believe this is the right action? What frames are they operating from?

This inches toward empathic understanding, naturally creating balanced conversations, judgments, and relationships. With more context, unpleasant actions become less grating. You see how they arrived at certain thoughts or actions, even if you don't agree with them. Trying to understand others better than they've tried to understand themselves puts you in a great position to navigate relationships.

REFLECTION QUESTIONS

The last piece of the self-survey section is a list of starter questions. If you've yet to try any exercises, now is the time to start. Look through the list, pick a question, and write down your answer. Repeat this for at least ten questions. While I recommend exploring additional tactics, this single exercise can serve as the foundation for your blueprint, which we'll discuss next.

Don't worry about crafting a perfect self-survey with amazing, polished answers. You can always tunnel further, answer more questions, or try other tactics later. The process is cyclical, not linear. The important part is starting. If you don't complete any exercises, you're missing much of the value in this framework.

- How do you spend most of your time each day?
- What activities do you most enjoy?
- What do you regularly do but dislike?
- What is the most challenging part of life right now?
- What upcoming event are you most excited about? Why?
- What is your ideal environment for solving problems?
- What are your natural talents?
- In what situations are you most anxious?
- In what situations are you most confident?
- What obstacles do you want to overcome? Why?
- What obstacles do you feel are insurmountable? Why?

➤ Have you challenged yourself lately? How?

➤ How do you feel about meeting new people?

➤ How do you feel about your social life?

➤ How do you feel about your romantic life?

➤ How are your relationships with loved ones?

➤ Are any relationships strained or difficult? Why?

➤ What do you expect from others in your life? Why?

➤ What do you expect from yourself? Why?

➤ How confident are you in handling conflict? Why?

➤ What are you most grateful for?

➤ Do you feel bitter or remorseful about anything? Why?

➤ How would you describe yourself?

➤ How would a close friend describe you?

➤ What are your most consistent habits?

➤ What would you rather die than give up?

➤ What could you sacrifice if you had to?

➤ What are your current goals?

➤ How do you feel about your career?

➤ How fulfilling is your work? Why?

➤ How do you feel about your finances?

➤ How do you feel about your physical health?

➤ What is the quality of your self-talk?

➤ What are you most proud of accomplishing? Why?

➤ What have you been procrastinating? Why?

➤ What are you most afraid of missing in life?

➤ Where do you feel most fulfilled?

➤ What have you learned lately?

- How would you describe your energy levels?
- What problems are recurring for you?
- What activities have you done most throughout your life?
- How do you spend your leisure time?
- What events cause you stress?
- How well do you handle stress?
- What drives you to work hard?
- How do you feel about yourself?
- Who do you admire? What does this admiration say about you?
- Who do you dislike? What does this dislike say about you?
- What habit do you most want to gain? Why?
- What habit do you most want to eliminate? Why?
- What emotions do you feel most often?
- What emotion is most difficult for you to manage?
- What topics have you been drawn to throughout life?
- What activities create the most desirable physical states?
- What activities create the most desirable emotional states?
- What activities create the most desirable purposeful states?
- What activities create the least desirable physical states?

- What activities create the least desirable emotional states?
- What activities create the least desirable purposeful states?
- What frames do you use most often?
- Which of your frames create positive evaluations?
- Which of your frames create negative evaluations?
- How often do you focus on states you can't change?
- How would you describe your relationship with control?

REFLECTION

The following set of questions is designed to help distill the ideas in this chapter. Take your time answering them and revisit any practices or exercises if you need to.

- How do you derive purpose in life?
- How do you derive pleasure in life?
- What are your common sources of desirable physical states? Emotional states? Meaningful states?
- What are the frequent sources of undesirable states for you?
- What are some of your frames around happiness?
- How well do you tune into and adjust focus?
- What factor most often blocks positive states for you?

- ➜ What recurring thought patterns do you have?

- ➜ What actions throughout your day feel habitual and automatic?

- ➜ What thoughts frequently surfaced in the last two weeks?

- ➜ How would you describe your life in regard to health, career, family, money, relationships, purpose, and growth?

- ➜ What are three of your strengths?

- ➜ What are three of your weaknesses?

- ➜ How do you spend time on a typical day? Have you tracked it?

4

CREATING A BLUEPRINT– PERSONAL VISION

magine overlooking your landscape again. It's a place you're now intimately familiar with. You're accustomed to the road's potholes, occasional flooding, and gardening cycles. You know where pathways lead and which ones you frequent. The layout is clear, but that's not the same as optimized.

The potholes are manageable, but they make travel difficult. The house is habitable, but space for an office would be nice. Knowing and accepting our current mindscape doesn't make life any easier, but it does improve our ability to wisely plan optimizations. We're now in a position to build a coherent plan for optimizing happiness.

Without a structured plan, we haphazardly work on whatever catches our attention. We scaffold a new room only to get distracted by floodproofing the cellar. Halfway through that, we start filling potholes instead. In the meantime, the scaffolding and half-built flood walls decay. No real progress happens. Having a clear strategy staves off distraction, keeping our focus on the most important projects.

That's where blueprints come into play. A blueprint, in this context, is your vision and plan for optimizing happiness. It's a refinement of who you want to be and what you want to accomplish. Most of us have a few shadowy ideas, but transforming those ideas into concrete, clear statements makes future decisions easy. This process takes some effort. How do we know what's most important? How can we develop our vision further? What if we don't have a personal vision?

Our self-survey provides excellent material for answering these questions. What does our survey say is most impactful? What creates unpleasant states and evaluations? What have we always cared about? We've already extracted relevant information; a blueprint is just the product of further distillation. Throughout this section, we'll cover the value of a blueprint, how to create one, and why you should update it periodically.

THE PURPOSE OF BLUEPRINTS

Your goal in creating a blueprint is codifying the values you believe most reliably produce desirable states and evaluations. You can then use those values to guide your goals and actions. You may make mistakes along the way, but over time, you can expect these choices to increasingly produce desirable outcomes.

The values you choose are your most important beliefs. They guide other decisions. When functioning properly, they improve your life. Poorly chosen values do exactly the opposite. In that case, the following questions naturally arise: *Which values are best for me? What should I base important decisions on? How should I live to optimize happiness?*

MULTIPLE SYSTEMS WORK

Early attempts to answer the previous questions left me baffled. How could similar lifestyles and beliefs produce different happiness levels? *Who was right? What determines happiness? Is it random?*

After a lot of searching, I found mostly contradictions and edge cases. There was some overlap, but not enough to produce a complete, coherent value system. I was working from a flawed premise during this search. A far simpler explanation exists. There is no perfect value system. Individual interests, upbringing, experience, and genetics are too varied to unify everyone around a single set of values. That doesn't mean values are useless, it means they must be personalized. They need to fit the contours of our mindscape.

Reconsidering our metaphor helps. Say you own a piece of land and want to build a house. What is the best style? Ranch, modern, colonial, wonderland, or something else? In this scenario, it's easy to recognize that there's no best aesthetic; they're all equally viable. It comes down to personal preference.

Choosing values to optimize happiness operates similarly. I can't dictate what's important to you, and I don't know which beliefs are most likely to produce desirable outcomes for you. I can, however, provide guidelines and tools for refining ideas. This should ease the process of choosing your own, personally optimized values. That's the focus of this chapter.

PICKING RELIABLE VALUES

Optimized values guide us toward actions that reliably produce desirable outcomes. Any value outside this definition should be updated or replaced. Consciously chosen values are relatively reliable; it's implicit values that tend to cause problems. These values are not chosen consciously, but they guide our actions nonetheless. It takes effort to ensure both our implicit and explicit values align with our desired actions and outcomes.

All values create some happiness. The question is, at what cost? Take elitism, for example, which produces pleasurable emotional and purposeful states when we judge ourselves better than others. At the same time, elitism also produces antisocial behaviors, sabotaging potential relationships. Relationships tend to be more valuable in producing desirable outcomes than individual, short-lived emotions, so elitism is a generally ineffective value.

Elitism may seem like a strange example. No one wakes up and says, "I want to be elitist today." Yet, plenty of people act that way. It's a common implicit value, with the frame *being better than others makes me valuable* guiding thoughts and actions. This is why self-survey is so important. Without it, we're unaware of the values determining our quality of life.

> Choosing better values starts with awareness.
> From there, you can determine effectiveness.

All effective values share common characteristics. Mainly, they are reliable and produce desirable outcomes. Reliable values are both controllable and clear. Effective values produce net positive trade-offs. Let's examine each characteristic more closely.

Controllable values use an internal yardstick, instead of allowing external forces to dictate alignment. For example, the value *I want others to like me* is mostly beyond our control. It's highly likely some subset of people, even if it's just a small percentage, won't like you no matter what you do. If you choose this value, your happiness is vulnerable to external circumstances. Any value beyond your control isn't reliable.

Many external values can be shifted internally with a frame adjustment. A controllable reframe of this value is *I treat everyone with compassion, empathy, and respect.* These behaviors generally produce likability and are within your control. There's no dependency on outside forces, which makes it far more reliable than *I want others to like me*.

Reliable values are also clear, acting as guidelines for behavior across many circumstances. Unclear values provide no such guidance because they are vague, well-intentioned ideas with no tangible use. This doesn't mean others need to understand your values, but they should definitely be clear to you.

Let's take vitality as an example. What does it mean? What actions can you take to enact vitality? Does it mean eating healthy, exercising, and getting enough sleep? Does it mean curating an engaging social calendar? Or something else entirely? All associations are valid, but effective values connect to your behaviors. Values should have a personal meaning. If you're considering a value that sounds nice but doesn't improve your decision-making, keep looking.

Finally, effective values improve your overall state, frame, or focus. While there may be unpleasant moments throughout the process, the payout should be a net positive. For example, taking a few months of communication classes to build your relationships can improve a lifetime of subsequent interactions. Another example is cutting out the momentary pleasure of junk food to improve the many states associated with your health. We could also trade state intensity, like in "adventure", by giving up physical or emotional comfort for more powerful meaning. Each of these is a net positive in desirability.

Trade-offs are an inherent part of selecting values. Time, attention, and resources are limited. Even if we only choose from effective values, we still need to determine our priorities. If we resonate with love more than achievement, it makes sense to forgo a great job for increased family time. If stability outweighs ambition, relaxed projects are preferable to risky ones. There are no right answers here. Instead, focus on the process of determining which value mix best fits your mindscape, weeding out net negatives along the way.

ACTUALIZING VALUES: HABITS AND GOALS

Values are only made tangible through action. Honesty, for example, can't exist in a vacuum. At the same time, explicitly comparing every choice against values is too cumbersome. Instead, we can use goals and habits as condensed abstractions for implementing value-based actions. This allows us to bundle desirable behaviors into manageable chunks, eliminating the overhead of individual comparisons.

Habits and goals may seem like simple concepts, but the two are often confused. The timeline is the key difference. Habits continue indefinitely while goals have clear completion criteria. Applying either tool to the wrong type of project produces inefficient frames and lackluster results.

Diets are commonly confused in this way. Most of us diet by setting goals like "I'll eat less this month, or I'll follow this diet until I lose 5lbs." Then we struggle, slowly inching our way toward completing the goal. That's where the plan ends: "Once I lose 5lbs, I can eat normally again." Wait. Isn't "eating normally" the set of habits that led to the original concern? If your actions change temporarily, your results will be temporary as well.

Meaningful diet changes to improve your health require habit change, not just short-term eating decisions. Yet, switching focus to a phrase like "I'll *always* eat healthily" likely feels hollow and overwhelming. The shift is drastic, vague, and probably unrealistic. How long before your willpower cracks and old habits return?

Luckily, there's a happy middle ground that combines the two. We can set incremental goals that build toward desirable, indefinite habits. Blending habits and goals allows us to slowly make desirable choices the default, with clear victories along the way. We don't have to completely commit to always eating healthy, but we can start working toward it. When tied to reliable values, this combination provides clear routes for optimizing happiness.

The process might look like this:

—*Health is one of my values.*

—*What habits create health?*

—*Clean eating supports my value of health.*

—*What is clean eating?*

—More vegetables, less processed food, and fewer sweets.

—What goals support clean eating?

—I'll only eat out once a week. I'll eat at least one serving of vegetables at every meal. After a successful month, I'll consider new health goals.

Here we've identified a value, tied it to a desirable habit, and identified clear actions for building that habit. This is essentially the core of blueprint creation. We're taking nebulous values we think will make us happy and refining them into specific action steps. We'll discuss the specifics of implementing those steps later. For now, let's focus on creating a blueprint from our values, habits, and goals.

VALUES FIRST

While brainstorming blueprint ideas, goals may come to mind more easily than values. This is normal, especially in the beginning. Most of us have spent far more time considering goals and habits than values, so we aren't as familiar with the terrain. Don't worry, goals alone can be used to start a blueprint. Just keep in mind that uncovering values is the eventual goal, as they're more reliable in optimizing happiness.

Goals are domain focused, which limits the number of viable pathways. Values are much broader and encompassing, providing countless options. For example, the value of extending human knowledge includes goals like discovering alien life or curing cancer, just to name a few. By anchoring your blueprint with values, you can better adapt to life's inevitable curveballs. New goals can always be created to fulfill a value.

Blueprints anchored to specific goals lose that flexibility. If your purpose and happiness hinge on curing cancer, a few risks arise. First, goals often have external factors that determine whether or not we achieve them. No one knows exactly how much work or what steps it will take to cure cancer, otherwise it would be done. It could happen tomorrow or in five hundred years. Second, goals are one-time events. If it never happens, you may feel regret and anguish. Third, most pathways can be blocked or disappear for reasons beyond your control. If someone discovers a cure first, your goal dissolves.

Beyond the initial roadblocks, actually achieving a life-long goal can also be frustrating. You may briefly be happy, but how long until you feel a lack of purpose? Having achieved one specific goal, what's next? Not feeling content often further compounds negative states with frustration. Regardless of how well you perform relative to your goals, goal-based blueprints have many potential pitfalls. Values are far more flexible.

One helpful frame is contrasting who you want to be (values) with what you want to do (habits and goals). Who you are cannot be directly modified by external influences because you always maintain some level of control over your actions. You can't, however, always choose what options are available. Making goals subservient to values shifts more happiness determinants into your control.

Revisiting the mindscaping metaphor, a values-first approach is the equivalent of planning a forest before planting individual trees. A goals-based approach is like focusing exclusively on one tree. If that tree becomes diseased or struck by a natural disaster, you'll be devastated. If your plan is a forest, however, you'll know you can plant more trees. It might be unpleasant if a tree you've been trying to grow catches fire, but you'll at least know other options exist.

As you work through the following exercises, try attaching your goals to corresponding values. As usual, tunneling is useful here. If you want to learn how to dance, ask what value it satisfies for you. If that's too difficult, try shifting into other questions, like "why do you want to dance?" Artistic expression? Physical fitness? Mastery of new skills?

It's alright if your first round of blueprint drafting doesn't produce perfect, polished value statements. You can still implement the rest of the framework. You'll bring more experience and clearer ideas into each successive round. You'll also have data about which actions and values most resonated in practice, which isn't always aligned with your initial assumptions. It takes time to refine an accurate, focused blueprint.

STARTING YOUR BLUEPRINT

We've covered what blueprints are, but what are the tactics for creating them? Our task is deceptively difficult. We need to decide what specific values, goals, and habits most consistently produce happiness. *What does a good life look and feel like? What guidelines will get me there?*

There's no shortage of opinions on how to live your best life. "You should never drink alcohol. You ought to contribute to charity. Become a doctor, lawyer, or engineer. Make lots of friends. Cultivate work-life balance. You really should care about the environment." Everywhere we turn, we're bombarded by potential blueprint components. Most of us have tacitly accepted some combination of these external components without examining how they fit with our mindscape.

Unfortunately, this rarely works out. Choosing components based on others' preferences almost always produces blueprint mismatches which are weakly or completely uncorrelated with happiness. These components tend to crumble under tunneling. For example:

—I need to get married before thirty.

—Why?

—It's something my parents keep bringing up. I've always wanted it.

—Why do you want it?

—*I don't want to be alone for the rest of my life.*

—*That seems reasonable, but is that outcome predetermined? Is thirty the cut-off for marriage?*

—*No. I can work toward getting married. I just want it before thirty.*

—*Is this timeline tied to a value?*

—*No, but the underlying value for being married is human connection.*

—*Is marriage the only way to fulfill human connection?*

—*No.*

This marriage timeline is an unrealistically constrained goal-based blueprint component.

How many of our beliefs are constructed this way? How often do we limit our happiness with rigid, unrealistic, goal-based blueprints? As you create your blueprint, examining the *why* behind each component is important. There is no "supposed to" or "should" when it comes to optimizing your happiness.

....

Don't pick ideas just because they're present. Tunnel to make sure they fit as well.

....

These gaps tend to become more visible during your self-survey, but we can enhance the process with intentional analysis. As you explore potential blueprint components, try distinguishing between those consciously chosen for optimization and those adopted merely through repeated exposure. Typically, those in the second bucket are rigid and happiness limiting. Values like "make my parents proud" sound nice, but are actually externally based and unreliable.

You are the architect of your life vision. You are the one who lives through your choices. Your past, others' expectations, or societal norms shouldn't dictate decisions unless they also optimize happiness. While external pressures are legitimate, you choose whether or not to apply those pressures internally. It may take time to dismantle, but ultimately each of us is in control of our own blueprint.

If you haven't thought about your personal vision before, start with first principles. Ignore your current circumstances and imagine the life you'd want if no one was judging you, you felt fully confident, and had unlimited resources. If you can tie that life into values-based statements, even better. This ideal life provides a simple baseline from which to extend.

The following tactics are meant for exploring potential configurations of blueprint components. Don't feel like you need to combine them all. The purpose of these exercises is to provide you with enough options that some resonate. Your focus should be on creating the most useful possible document(s) for yourself. As always, feel free to personalize and modify for mindscape fit.

EXAMPLE BLUEPRINT

Each blueprint configuration is unique, but seeing an example can help clarify the intended result. You do not need these specific structures in your blueprint. I'm just sharing what happens to work for me, for illustrative purposes. My blueprint contains three sections:

List of Value Statements

- ➔ I prioritize my mental and physical health.
- ➔ I treat everyone with kindness, an open mind, and respect.
- ➔ I am grateful, present, and grounded.
- ➔ I engage with each day to expand my knowledge, skill, or experience.
- ➔ I stay organized, focused, and tidy.

My blueprint orbits around five core values. While they may seem simple, creating this list took three years of gradual refinement. In each iteration, my values have been adjusted, more accurately guiding me toward desirable states and evaluations. While the list feels complete right now, there's a chance I'll make further refinements next time I comb through.

This list alone, however, is useless without accompanying actions. Every night, I contemplate my choices throughout the day. How did I struggle or excel in making choices aligned with these values? I then tunnel through those answers for future, optimized adjustments. My choices are nowhere near perfect, but I'm always working toward living these values more completely.

For example, perhaps I make a snide comment about a coworker. I would later compare this event to the value of treating everyone with kindness, an open mind, and respect. Clearly, this action isn't in line with my values. Next, I tunnel through my decision. *Why did I say that? What was I hoping to accomplish?* Most likely, my answer is something like: *It was a habitual judgment. I didn't think through the consequences.*

Then I might tunnel through the impact of acting this way in the future. *How might this habit hinder my happiness?* The coworker may hear about what I said, damaging the relationship. The person I commented to may see me as rude and gossipy. They may become more guarded, wondering how I speak about them to others. Also, making this comment didn't create a more desirable state for me than kindness would have. Overall, there's only a potential loss in happiness with no upside.

This example may seem time-consuming for such a trivial event. I've found, however, that small, frequent reflections allow fast course-correction. *Are my daily frames and choices boosting or hindering my happiness?* Over time, these reflections also create a library of knowledge about how my daily choices impact my happiness. It doesn't guarantee perfect future choices, but constant nudges in the right direction certainly make an impact.

Mission Statement

The second component in my blueprint is a mission statement derived from the previous values. I recreate this mission statement each year to encapsulate my aspirations. I cap the length to one sentence, for brevity. Again, not a necessity, just what resonates with me.

My mission statement for the year is: Document the theoretical foundations for my future happiness projects. I review this statement every day to ensure at least one action is aligned with that aspiration. This is more of a goal-based blueprint component, but it connects with the values of staying focused and engaging with each day to expand knowledge.

One-Year Goal Calendar

The last component in my blueprint is a one-year calendar derived from my values and mission statement. This calendar begins with broad yearly goals, which are then broken down into more specific quarterly goals. The quarterly goals are again broken down into monthly goals. Those are often broken down even further, reaching the point of daily actions.

As you might imagine, this creates a rather lengthy set of goals and subgoals. I won't bore you with the full details, plus this draws heavily on implementation information, which we'll discuss later. To give you some idea, however, here's a pseudo-one-month goal list:

- ➜ Edit thirty pages.
- ➜ Create four short happiness-based videos.
- ➜ Reach out to thirty content creators for guest blog appearances.
- ➜ Read two books.
- ➜ Finish one supplemental psychology course: "Habit Change."

The first goal was derived from a quarterly goal (finish the second draft of this book), which came from the yearly goal (finish and release this book). It's relatively easy to continually subdivide top-level goals until you reach weekly and daily goals. This process also naturally produces metrics for tracking long-term projects. I can trace individual actions back to the specific values they were extracted from. We'll circle back to this in the implementation chapter.

An Example, Not a Template

These three components comprise my blueprint. If it seems somewhat polished, it's only because I experimented substantially over the years to determine what works for me. The components will almost certainly continue to evolve as I'm exposed to life changes and new tools. I hope it helps generate a few ideas for your blueprint.

That being said, your blueprint may look similar or completely different than mine. It may have a single component, or seven. The specifics aren't important, only that the components improve consistency in taking happiness-optimizing actions. Also, I highly recommend actually creating a blueprint while reading this chapter as you'll find it is useful in later chapters.

BLUEPRINT CREATION TACTICS

As we shift into blueprint creation tactics, keep in mind the importance of self-acceptance and idealism during this process. Use the height of your aspirations without limits. Create the most jaw-dropping landscape you can envision. It may sound cliche, but many accomplishments hinge on imagination and self-belief. We're far more likely to enact action when we first see it in our mind's eye.

Another reminder: Regardless of the distance to your aspirations, there is no "good" or "bad" starting position. Unlike goals, values have no endpoint. Focus on creating guidelines for the type of person you want to be *ideally* and *eventually.* You don't need to drastically force change by tomorrow, this month, or even this year. Being kind to others is a position we can always work toward. The beginning doesn't matter because the process has no end.

Cars are a good parallel. The engine in a van, semi-truck, and sports car can all be improved for speed. The sportscar is likely fastest at the outset, but that doesn't change the possibility of making it faster. All three types can be made faster, indefinitely. In addition, if you spend years improving the speed of one, it will eventually match or outpace the other two. The starting point has influence, but the process is far more important for outcomes.

In a similar spirit, your starting point is likely to be far less relevant than it feels. There are no first places, no bests, and no perfect. There is only an optimization process based on your desired outcomes. Focus on who you want to be and what you can control. That's where you'll make progress. Regardless of where you are now, approaching these exercises with imagination and idealism will produce the best results.

VALUES LIST

The simplest tactic is just creating a list of values. Most of us already know our values, to some degree, and this is a sufficiently useful starting point. While the initial list may be too long, vague, or external, it can always be further refined. A large portion of blueprints use this list as the cornerstone and build from there.

Completing this tactic is relatively easy. Just write a list of values at the level of detail that makes sense to you. Choosing values that are a great fit, however, is a bit harder. As a reminder, ideal values are internally driven, guide decisions toward happiness, and apply to many situations.

I also recommend being concise, where possible. Concise values are typically more comprehensible, easier to remember verbatim, and easier to incorporate into daily life. It's also faster to review them daily. More than ten values tend to be cumbersome and difficult to remember. As always, mold the tactic to fit your mindscape. For most, however, a long list produces more overhead than results.

A list of values can take many forms, but here are a few common styles.

Single Words

The most commonly effective arrangement is a list of individual words. They are concise, broadly applicable, and easily communicable. In addition, example lists abound, making it easy to pick and choose from a series of options.

Single words are also easy to remember. For example, an acquaintance has "love" as their sole value. It's pretty easy to gauge your actions against that metric. Most people, however, need a few more to cover more situations. I know someone who uses "humor, knowledge, stability, balance, and growth" and another that prefers "honesty, family, education, kindness and inner harmony." These are all good options. If this style resonates with you, it's a common and convenient choice.

A List of Value-Based Sentences

If you find single words too generic or disembodied, then using full sentences may be a better fit. This style trades concision for additional context and specificity. Value-based sentences also tend to be more personal, as few people adopt the exact same phrases. With this personalization, many also find it easier to compare against daily decisions. In creating value-based sentences, short, generalized statements tend to work best.

Here's an example:

- ➜ I'm loving to everyone I know and meet.
- ➜ I complete whatever I set my mind to.
- ➜ I better myself physically, emotionally, and mentally each day.
- ➜ I explore my curiosities from a stable baseline.

Each sentence covers a broad range of activities, crafted in unique, personalized language. Occasionally, however, sentences can become too constrained. As you draft ideas, brainstorm potential goals for each value. Imagining a few options should be easy. Otherwise, your statement is likely to be too constrained. Following this guideline provides more structure than individual words while ensuring the statements are broad enough to be used as values.

Paragraph(s)

Finally, you can detail your values in a paragraph (or several). As opposed to the other styles, paragraph values tend to form a single coherent statement instead of isolated, individual guidelines. As with previous tactics, the ideal value paragraph is both concise and all-encompassing.

Here's an example of paragraph-style values:

I strive to be the best version of myself. That means treating people and animals well, chasing my passions, staying healthy, and doing what is right. I constantly monitor my behavior to ensure I'm living in line with these values. This ensures I make progress while enjoying life, which is my ultimate aspiration.

Paragraph-style values tend to be the clearest and most readable, as there's additional context. The primary downfall is they can become burdensome to review. If your values start expanding beyond a single paragraph, you may want to look for shorthand ways to review them regularly. Otherwise, checking values daily can become too time consuming.

Regardless of style, a good litmus test for values is comparing them against your actions today. How well do they guide you toward optimizing states and evaluations? Ideally, your values allow you to tunnel through any situation to analyze decisions and outcomes. For example, *I didn't apply for that promotion. That action goes against my value of Bravery. What can I change to align my actions with that value? I did great eating nutritious food today. What made it easy to choose Health today? How can I do it in the future?*

Finding values that reliably create desirable states is harder than it seems at first glance. It usually takes time and several iterations. Don't worry if your initial values don't seem perfect. Part of the process is testing them against life to see which ones actually produce desirable outcomes. As usual, getting the process right is far more important than the outcome.

MISSION STATEMENT

Mission statements are another common potential blueprint component. A mission statement is simply a declaration of an aspiration, usually in a few sentences or less. While this may seem similar to paragraph-style values, mission statements typically encapsulate value-based accomplishments instead of traits.

If you want to create a mission statement, start by answering this question: What do I want to accomplish in life?

Hundreds of projects, skills, and minor curiosities may come to mind, but work to extract the highest-level common theme. For example, I strive to optimize happiness in myself and others by using, creating, and sharing tools. In their best form, lifelong mission statements can be achieved through multiple routes. The previous example could be satisfied by writing books, sharing resources made by others, testing software, etc.

You can also create time-boxed mission statements, as I've done in my blueprint. When you add a timeline, however, you shift away from values toward goals. This means increasing specificity, thus narrowing the number of routes to achievement. If you choose this route, try to also link to another blueprint component, which contains higher-level values.

As with values, a clear and concise mission statement is easiest to review. That being said, it's more important that your statement guides your actions toward desirable outcomes. Many mission statements are a single sentence, but don't hesitate to write more if it better encapsulates your aspirations.

LIFESTYLE PROJECTION

Value lists and mission statements leave much to interpretation, particularly the interactions between choices and outcomes. Lifestyle projections, on the other hand, provide a clear, simple mapping between the two. Lifestyle projections are generally good blueprint components, but especially useful for those who find the previous tactics too airy.

A lifestyle projection boils down to creating an average day in your ideal life. We choose an average day because phrases like "the best day ever" tend to create unsustainable long-term ideas. Our goal here is to create a practical, tangible view of your ideal happiest life. You can then use that picture as an endpoint to guide daily decisions.

Start by describing the flow of your ideal average day from waking to resting. It's typically easiest to visualize each part, then write the details afterward. Here's an example:

I wake up promptly at 6:30 a.m., feeling well-rested. Sun bleeds through the curtains, along with a light breeze. It's a warm day, and I'm in a medium-sized North American city. I look out the window, enjoying the view of lush greenery for a few moments. I walk outside to the porch and settle into my daily fifteen-minute meditation . . .

Visualizing an entire day takes time, but it also provides abundant information for crystalizing desirable actions. The exercise brings each moment to life, providing concrete representations of how you'll feel and act when life is most desirable. You can then reverse-engineer ideal states, distilling goals, and habits from your projections.

For example, "I wake up promptly at 6:30 a.m. feeling well-rested" implies habits of quality rest and starting the day early. If those aren't already habits, they can be set as intentions for your blueprint. You can work through your entire visualization this way, creating habits and goals from practically every sentence.

By continually working through these reverse-engineered goals, life increasingly mirrors the projection. As the gap closes, you can repeat the exercise, updating parts of your ideal day based on your new circumstances. It's guaranteed that as you make progress, your needs will also evolve, opening new paths to optimizing happiness. Unlike values, each projection is a snapshot for guiding development, instead of an overarching lifelong trait.

Projections are powerful and useful, but there are a few common hiccups. The first is that projections often have serious gaps. For example, you may not know your ideal job or where you want to live. Placeholders can help you find the answer, but their guidance may be cloudy.

For example, you might write: "I work for five hours a day at [something]" during the visualization stage. When later creating goals, you can fill this gap with something like "try three types of work for at least one month each." Alternatively, you can use other exercises to supplement your projection or focus exclusively on parts of the projection which are clear. Regardless, you can move forward without mapping out every detail.

Choosing a specific future time for your projection requires nuance as well. It's unlikely one ideal day captures your entire life from childhood to old age. Most people can intuitively pick a period without much trouble, but not everyone considers the consequences. Your choice influences all associated goals. The timeline has implications for what you'll end up prioritizing.

For example, your original projection might be five years away and include having a child. A projection twenty years from now will include a teenager instead. An ideal day with an infant will differ drastically from one with a teenager. Your projection may create different guideposts for making decisions. There's no correct timeline; it's just something to be cognizant of when using this tactic.

One last note, lifestyle projections beyond ten years are likely to change significantly. It might make more sense to project an additional, intermediate period and focus there. Maybe your long-term projection includes having a child.

Before that, you'll likely want a partner and a stable, loving relationship. These precedent steps each contain the potential for complete projections. This subdivision makes it easier to extract short-term goals and actions, which then feed into the longer-term projection.

LEGACY REVIEW

Another tactic similar to projection is the legacy review. A legacy review outlines the reputation, achievements, and experiences you aspire to before death. While considering mortality may feel morbid, our lives are inevitably limited. Considering this reality highlights what's most important in life, which leads to optimizing happiness. For this reason, many people find creating values easiest when considering their legacy.

A legacy review typically has three core components:

- Reputation
- Achievements
- Experiences

Reputation equates to character traits and values, while achievements and experiences are fairly self-explanatory. To create a legacy review, write your desired outcomes in each realm. For some, it helps to think of it as a eulogy. Here's an example:

I want to be remembered for adding positivity to everyone around me. To be known for being generous and kind. To have provided for my family while being patient and understanding.

Continue until you've completely covered the type of person you want to be remembered as. After finishing reputation, you can move into accomplishments and experiences. If it helps, consider this as an expanded bucket list, encapsulating everything you want to accomplish in life. The result might look like this:

> Before my life is over, I'd like to earn a master's degree in physics. I want to get married and have children. I'd like to own a business and travel to at least fifteen countries.

Once you've transcribed your entire desired legacy, compare it against your current actions. Are your actions guiding you toward this outcome? If not, what can you change to get there? Again, you can work to reverse engineer your desired outcomes. Projections of each component can help guide your future decisions to optimize happiness.

TRAITS OF ASPIRATIONAL PEOPLE

Not everyone is clear about who they want to be or what they want to accomplish. With endless options, it's hard to pick just a handful. If you're in that position, don't worry. The next few tactics are designed for the common problem of a fuzzy future vision. The first tactic we'll cover is deriving values from traits of aspirational figures.

You may not know exactly what you want, but it's almost guaranteed you admire certain individuals. These can be historical figures, celebrities, personal acquaintances, or even fictional characters. Understanding why you admire these individuals provides great clues for discovering values you'll find compelling.

To start this exercise, list anyone who has earned your admiration. Next, write the traits and/or accomplishments you admire about each person. Once you've completed the list, scan the entries for overlapping themes. If a trait appears multiple times, it's likely meaningful. For example, you might come up with something like this:

- ➔ Lincoln—strong, uniting, **passionate**
- ➔ Einstein—**passionate**, intelligent, outspoken
- ➔ Mother Teresa—kind, **passionate**, genuine

Passion is repeated throughout the list. Accordingly, it's likely to be a value that resonates. This example is simple, but it shows how the process generally works. You'll want to add detail when actually completing the exercise. Try tunneling into your choices for additional context. The goal is to extract at least a few potential goals or values by the end.

It's important to note that this tactic isn't about comparison with, mirroring, or surpassing others. Instead, the intention is to use impressions of others to better understand yourself. You're drilling into your core values to develop internal, reliable ideas for guiding action. Measuring yourself against others leaves your happiness vulnerable to negative thoughts, like *I'm not measuring up* or *I'll never accomplish anything like they did.*

....

Your path will be different. Use what you admire in others to build your own blueprint.

....

BORROW FROM OTHERS' BLUEPRINTS

This may seem contradictory to the previous section, but the next tactic is borrowing directly from others' blueprints. Many well-established, respected individuals' blueprints are documented and publicly available. These are great sources of inspiration. The key to useful borrowing is cherry-picking only ideas that deeply resonate with you, without copying anyone exactly.

One of the most well-known blueprints is Benjamin Franklin's thirteen values, which he used for personal character development. I won't include them all here, for the sake of space, but they're easy to find. The list includes values like temperance and frugality. This is just one example of the many public blueprints you can draw from in creating your own blueprint.

This tactic is especially useful for those having trouble with their first draft. You can explore other blueprints, cobbling together pieces that fit your mindscape. Over time, you can iterate on these components and further personalize them. This is valuable because values copied verbatim are typically less relevant than those in your own words. Each word in your blueprint should be personally relevant. Rarely is that found in someone else's vision, even if just copying a small portion.

Think of it like building a table. Would you feel more ownership following step-by-step instructions or crafting your own design with personal touches? Creating your blueprint is similar. You may need to borrow steps to build your first table, but as your familiarity with the topic increases, creating your own will produce a more gratifying outcome.

DOUBLE DOWN ON YOUR STRENGTHS

We're all naturally good at some subset of tasks, whether by genetics or experience. If we don't have contradictory aspirations, doubling down on our strengths can be a useful blueprint component. As a bonus, this tactic is especially easy after completing a self-survey, as time has been spent tunneling on strengths and weaknesses.

The primary benefit of using your strengths as a blueprint component is that you're likely to succeed at associated goals. If nothing else seems more meaningful, your natural talents are an easy path to continue exploring. By further exploring your talents, you're likely to encounter new, enjoyable opportunities. You can always explore other options later if your strengths don't seem to bring joy.

For this exercise, list your strengths in terms of accomplishments, traits, or tendencies. Try to be as broad as possible, so there's a chance of uncovering values as well. If you did any of this work in the previous section, feel free to reuse it with this new frame. When you're done, it might look like this:

Empathy

→ Have a master's degree in psychology
→ Be a counselor as a career
→ Volunteer twice a month

Intellectual Curiosity

→ Read a book a month
→ Complete a three-month set of cooking classes
→ Intentionally talk to new people about their lives

Writing

→ Have written four books
→ Write blog posts bi-weekly
→ Write poetry occasionally

This is just one example. Exploring strengths can take many forms. After listing information, however, you'll want to search for connections between actions, aspirations, and successes. Often, these connections will be values. If not, you can also use past strengths to guide future goals. They may not be all-encompassing values, but it's definitely a useful starting point. You can always evolve the ideas later.

You may be wondering why weaknesses weren't mentioned, so let's unpack why strengths are the logical choice. Weaknesses are, by definition, traits that require extra work for us to become competent. Why pour effort into marginal returns when strengths produce better outcomes? It makes sense to leverage investments with the best outcomes.

Some may argue, "My weaknesses prevent me from doing X and make me feel Y." This is a slightly different case. If weaknesses limit happiness, they're worth working on. Most of the time, however, this doesn't require work on the weaknesses themselves, but on the associated frames.

If your particular aspirations require working through weaknesses, the path is clear. This tactic is aimed at those still trying to determine their blueprint. If nothing in your blueprint indicates working on a weakness will optimize happiness, it makes more sense to invest that time into your strengths. Working on weaknesses without a related value creates unnecessary difficulty without any corresponding gain.

Think of it as installing a pool in the desert. If you don't plan to use the pool, it makes sense to build some other desert-friendly feature instead. There's no reason to expend extra effort on a feature you don't care about, don't like, and won't use. It might feel impressive, but how does it improve your life? And yet many still feel pressured to work on their weaknesses. I, for example, am particularly bad at house maintenance. Yet, I often feel the need to bungle my way through home repairs. This is a deeply habitual, unreliable blueprint component that says, "I should complete tasks myself, without help." Whenever I catch this frame, I tunnel through it, questioning its usefulness. This is usually enough to stop me from choosing undesirable outcomes and hire a specialist instead.

To be clear, I'm not recommending avoiding weaknesses or challenges. I'm mainly saying effort should focus on opportunities likely to optimize happiness. Optimization often involves working on difficult tasks and fortifying weaknesses. Working on weaknesses simply for the sake of working on weaknesses, however, doesn't provide much value.

TRY NOVELTY

There's a chance you've gotten this far without generating any blueprint ideas. Perhaps you're not sure what values, goals, or habits will increase happiness. With practically infinite options, it's hard to pin down just a few. Don't worry if you don't yet see a clear future direction, it's very common. In that situation, consider starting your blueprint with novelty, focusing on exploring new experiences.

The idea of "following your passion" as the key to happiness is rather pervasive. Not only is this platitude vague and naive, but many of us don't even have an all-consuming passion. Advice focuses on "chasing your dreams," with little talk of how to discover them. This makes some individuals feel like they're the only ones without a passion, creating existential dread.

The reality is few of us have crystal clear, passion-driven plans for our lives. More often, our first blueprint works until we graduate from school, give or take a few years, then is shattered by the realities of life: "I always wanted to be a lawyer, but I hate this path. I don't know what's next." Feeling like you've picked the wrong path is common and can strike at any point in life. Unfortunately, this feeling rarely comes with a clear picture of what to do next.

When you're unsure of how to increase your happiness, you can focus your blueprint on increasing variety. By trying new activities, you can experience new states with differing levels of desirability. You can then compare them, figuring out what's worth pursuing and what should be left behind. Most importantly, you gain actual experience instead of speculating on what actions optimize happiness.

Start this exercise by creating a value such as, "I regularly try new activities to better understand myself and what brings me happiness." This will anchor your blueprint. Next, brainstorm activities you're willing to try: skydiving, martial arts, weaving, songwriting, blogging, reselling, etc. Again, anything you're willing to try, not just those activities you want to try. The final list will be broad, and possibly unrelated, but that's the point.

From that list, you can develop concrete goals. For example, perhaps you'll attend a class on one of the topics each month. Or spend three hours each week exploring a topic. It's not about completely rewriting your current life; it's about dedicating time to exploration. For most, the biggest hurdle is actually taking action as opposed to simply contemplating what might be nice.

As you explore new experiences, tunnel through them. Ask:

→ What did I learn about myself?
→ How might this activity add to my life?
→ How did I feel during and after it?

This process can clarify your self-survey and help generate a robust blueprint. Lived experiences are far better predictors of happiness than imagining what an activity might be like. If you're not sure what else to work on, simply explore what life and the world have to offer.

NOVELTY FOR THE COMPLETE BLUEPRINT

Novelty can also be useful for those at the other end of the spectrum who feel life is perfectly aligned with their blueprint. Since we only ever experience a fraction of what's possible, other states or frames may be even more desirable. While there's no serious pressure to change if you're happy, novelty clarifies blueprints in the same way that exploring philosophy clarifies values. While you might hit diminishing returns, there's always a chance you'll find something significantly useful.

It's like buying from the same store for years with no concerns. The store is great for your needs. One day, you decide to try another, closer store. You realize the products are of higher quality and less expensive. You've been content shopping at the first store, but exploring has yielded a better option. It's not a revolutionary or necessary change, but even marginal benefits count in optimization.

Novelty also prepares us for the inevitability of change. Becoming too accustomed to the status quo leaves us vulnerable to even small changes. We forget how to adapt or lose sight of alternatives. Exploring novelty keeps alternatives fresh in your mind. If your current blueprint is blocked or otherwise interrupted, adjusting is easier. We'll cover accepting change in depth later, but for now, just know that novelty improves adaptability.

LIFE CATEGORIES (AND A BLUEPRINT PRIMER)

Our last tactic for this chapter is called **"life categories"**. This involves creating buckets correlating to major life realms (or values), then adding related goals. For many, life realms feel more concrete than words like "passion". This tactic directly ties goals into the aspect of life they improve.

The first step is deciding on your buckets. The next example uses the following categories:

→ Mental health
→ Physical health

- Finance
- Growth
- Relationships

These aren't rigid categories, as "philosophy" or "community" could easily be used instead. As with values, prioritize broad, encompassing realms over more specific ones. After deciding on your buckets, add goals and habits which would contribute to that realm. You can either add desired outcomes or specific goals. It might look something like this:

Mental: For my mental health, I want to be less stressed. I want to feel less anxious in new social settings....

Finances: In my financial life, I want to save for and purchase a home. I want to find a job I enjoy more...

Continue like this until you've filled each category. If aspirations feel vague, tunnel through them to create a more tangible sentence. In the end, you should have several ideas for actions that will directly improve your life.

It's worth noting that this tactic can make realms appear independent, which is rarely true. For example, learning to manage conflict could fall under both "relationships" and "mental health". A stress-relief course could fall under "mental health" and "physical health". Life rarely segments into neat little boxes. Categories are used to ease brainstorming and organization, not describe life as it is. Knowing how a goal optimizes happiness is far more important than assigning it to the right bucket.

Since this is the last tactic, I've added a list of concepts that generally increase happiness, but this is not intended to be prescriptive or comprehensive. I list topics only by name, but most have multiple books dedicated to them. Regardless of your blueprint progress, it's worth exploring these topics for their potential impact on your happiness.

MENTAL HEALTH

- Optimism and realistic/positive thinking
- Stress management
- Perception of control
- Gratitude practice
- Abundance mindset
- Growth mindset
- Independent self-assessment (not comparing with others or taking criticism as fact)
- Emotional regulation

PHYSICAL HEALTH

- Sleep patterns
- Exercise routine
- Diet and nutrition (long term, not quick fixes)
- Disease management/prevention (based on personal risk factors)

FINANCES

- ➜ How you spend money
- ➜ Budgeting
- ➜ How you make money
- ➜ Enjoying your work
- ➜ Increasing income
- ➜ Investing/passive income
- ➜ Your relationship with money

GROWTH AND PRODUCTIVITY

- ➜ Skill mastery (sports, art, etc.)
- ➜ Novel experiences (travel, moving abroad, classes, etc.)
- ➜ Meaning and purpose (philosophy, religion, etc.)
- ➜ Flow states
- ➜ Time management and organization
- ➜ Decluttering and minimalism

RELATIONSHIPS

- ➜ Active listening
- ➜ Clear communication (refining ideas regardless of medium)
- ➜ Acts of kindness practice
- ➜ Perspective-taking/empathy (putting yourself in others' shoes)
- ➜ Negotiation

UNDERSTANDING OTHER PEOPLE'S BLUEPRINTS

Blueprints are also useful in understanding others' motivations, thoughts, and actions more clearly. By understanding someone else's values, we see what drives them. While you won't always have the full picture, intuiting the quality of someone's values can tell us a lot about them.

This became clear to me during a recent interaction. I met a man, and within moments, it was evident he was obsessed with chasing women and making money. On the surface, these seem like shallow, unappealing values akin to elitism and not particularly engaging.

Listening to him further, the structure of his blueprint became clear: "Of course I took the job, when you come from a family like mine, it's embarrassing to make less than I do now. I hate the work, but at least I can afford name brands. That's what women like, and I don't feel like a loser. It's the only option."

Those few sentences spoke volumes. He wasn't shallow, but feeding perversions of values like "make my family proud, be confident in my worth, and enjoy interactions with others." Unfortunately, these values were manifest by implicit frames, like "I need to prove I'm better than others. I want to own expensive possessions and receive physical validation from women." His values and tactics were almost exclusively external and unreliable.

Understanding his blueprint didn't make him any more pleasant. It did, however, allow me to be more empathetic.

He didn't complete a self-survey, then consciously choose those values to build his blueprint. He wasn't aware of other paths that more reliably produce happiness. Instead, his blueprint was cobbled together from social pressure and past experiences, like most people's. Unfortunately, he absorbed uncontrollable values (external validation, comparison with others) with low effectiveness (we can't control others' actions, trying to be better than others undermines valuable relationships).

Instead of disliking him, I felt compassion. He's on a long, unfulfilling path, with no knowledge of how to optimize happiness. Any small spikes of happiness will be dictated almost exclusively by external circumstances. As a proponent of happiness, I wouldn't wish that on anyone. I can only hope he experiences enough undesirable states to dissolve those frames, allowing him to explore other, better options.

A FOGGY, SECONDHAND PATCHWORK

Unfortunately, the majority of blueprints are secondhand, ill-founded, and confused. There can be many reasons for this, including upbringing, unclear vision, fixed mindset, low confidence, weak values, or little reflection. Without the proper tools, it's unsurprising that many of us are generally unhappy. It's hard enough to execute a polished blueprint effectively, let alone a shoddy, happenstance one.

Few people spend significant time reflecting on their values. Even fewer know how to question, dissolve, and reconstruct full blueprints. That means most people use blueprints provided by their upbringing, authority figures, or past experiences, without much modification. These blueprints tend to be muddied, external, and short term, lacking guidance for determining what's worth pursuing. This makes happiness seem mostly random, fluttering in and out with the tides of chance.

The worst case produces unfulfilled individuals struggling to maintain any semblance of happiness, as their blueprints often lead to actions which only worsen their position. To make matters worse, constant unhappiness typically makes individuals difficult to interact with. This creates isolation and further unpleasant experiences, strengthening the downward spiral. If left unchecked, this can leave individuals with few tactics for creating happiness, most of which are unreliable, misguided, or even dangerous to themselves and others.

It's an unfortunate reality that so many are struggling. Yet, without exposure to tools for creating desirable outcomes, what else could be expected? You can't walk a path you don't know exists. When interacting with others, consider the foundation of their blueprint. While this may not make everyone enjoyable, it at least increases understanding and empathy. Many people don't understand the full implications of their actions or viable alternatives.

MAGNIFICENT MASTERPIECES

On the other hand, a small minority have polished, exquisite blueprints. These individuals know exactly who they are and what they want from life. They are almost always happy, successful (by their own definition), and magnetic. Clear blueprints provide confidence, which generally attracts and inspires others.

When you meet individuals with powerful blueprints, capitalize on the opportunity to learn from them. Your blueprints may differ, but analyzing their beliefs, strategies, and tactics is likely to yield useful insights. Don't copy specific values and desired outcomes. Instead, focus on the processes they use to create clarity in their lives. This allows you to leverage their experience in refining your own blueprint.

HAPPINESS IS A MORAL RELATIVIST

This section is a slight detour, but fairly important. It may sound like I'm evangelizing a particular set of morals. That's not my intention. There are circumstances where values you or I consider immoral can create reliable and genuine happiness. Had the unpleasant man in the previous example used money as a proxy for adding value to the world or womanizing because he enjoys intimate relationships, those same tactics might have proven fruitful in optimizing happiness. Happiness is rooted in fairly subjective state evaluations.

Consider those with extreme religious views. Many of these individuals are clear on who they are, their personal vision, and which actions fulfill their values. Yet their ideas might include extending truth through eradicating non-believers. While I find this morally dubious, the action is controllable and tied to a reliable value. That means it's just as likely to produce happiness as, say, universally optimizing happiness through writing books.

While there are strong arguments for actions that universally optimize happiness, morality is beyond the scope of this book. The truth is any reliable, controllable, and net-positive value tied to actions through strong enough frames can produce happiness, regardless of the impact on others or society as a whole. Whether certain values and actions are the *right* choices is another conversation entirely.

Fortunately, most antisocial behaviors have naturally negative consequences and require frames that are hard to rationalize. For example, eradicating non-believers not only contradicts the spirit of most religions and religious individuals but also makes retaliation likely. If the potential cost is death, there are almost certainly other, better routes to extending truth.

I don't mean to imply morality is unimportant, but to highlight how individuals may derive happiness from activities which seem immoral. Just as mindscapes differ, so can morals. Understanding an individual's blueprint means knowing how they chase happiness. Regardless of how you feel about their methods, they may effectively and reliably produce happiness. There are no right answers here, only guidelines for optimizing choices.

BLUEPRINTS ARE THE DESIGN

In this section, we've covered the importance of blueprints and how to create one. Grounding your future plans in clear, coherent values and visions makes creating concrete action steps easy. Once you know *who* you want to become, you can focus on *how*.

At this point, your blueprint probably isn't as polished as you'd like. That's to be expected. If, however, you haven't been able to start at all, consider taking a break from this book to investigate a few philosophical resources. These generally provide well-crafted, logical arguments for specific values, morals, and belief systems. Happiness isn't particular about the specifics, but some foundation for determining value is necessary.

Assuming a completed blueprint, we can shift our focus toward implementation. Before delving into action, however, we must develop the right frame of mind to follow through, even during difficult circumstances. The road between the present and future is long and almost certainly laced with challenges. Blueprints are powerless if we lose faith and motivation at the first hiccup. Accordingly, the next section is focused on building confidence and esteem. These form the foundation for tackling every other project of interest.

REFLECTION

The following set of questions is designed to help distill the ideas in this chapter. Take your time answering them and revisit any practices or exercises if you need to.

→ Where do you see yourself in five years?

→ Where do you see yourself in ten years?

→ What would life look like with no constraints?

→ How often do you write down or adjust goals?

→ When was the last time you set a clear, measurable goal?

→ What are your most important values?

→ How well do your goals tie into your values?

→ What is your current mission statement (or equivalent alternative)?

→ Who do you most admire? What do you admire about them?

→ How do you want your life to look in regards to health, career, family, money, relationships, purpose, and growth?

→ If you could change one aspect of your life, what would it be? How can you move toward that?

→ What would you like to accomplish in life?

→ What change would most increase your positive states?

→ What change would most decrease your negative states?

→ How can you change frames to produce more happiness?

→ Which of your beliefs do you need to challenge?

→ What is your biggest dream?

→ What does your perfect day look like?

5

HOMEBUILDING – CONFIDENCE AND ESTEEM

Imagine being dropped into a landscape where you'll spend the rest of your life. What feature would you build first? For most, shelter, or a home, is the answer that comes to mind. A home provides a safe, familiar, and private place where you can seek refuge and recovery. Without a home, other development is difficult. How can you recuperate from exhausting physical labor if you're sleeping on the ground? If you expect to develop other features, a home is a high priority.

Think of your mind in a similar way. Before accepting extra projects, you need a strong, stable foundation. In your mind, that foundation comes from strong habits of confidence and esteem. These provide the emotional resilience necessary to weather challenges and persevere. We'll discuss how to build these characteristics soon, but first, let's explore why they're so important.

BUILDING WITHOUT A HOME

Imagine you want to build a fence around your entire property. You plan on cutting down fifty trees to use as lumber. The next morning, you rise early, get your axe, start hacking and continue until completely exhausted. Every muscle aches as you slowly trudge home. You eagerly anticipate a much-needed night's rest.

Finally, you arrive back at your person-sized shack. The construction of your meager home is flimsy, with gaps and cracks everywhere, leaving you at the mercy of the elements and bugs. There's nothing inside, not even a mattress or pillow. In fact, there's no flooring whatsoever. Your only option is to sleep on the hard, uneven dirt. It's not much, but you're exhausted and attempt to get some sleep.

You awake the next day feeling unrested. However, you're still determined to build a fence, so you head out to collect more lumber. After another day of effort, you make some progress, but less than yesterday. Residual tiredness takes its toll, causing you to return home earlier. Conditions at home haven't improved, though. For the second night, you only manage a few hours of sleep.

Several days into this process, you start feeling ill. Without sleep or relaxation, the physical burden has increased to the point that your body can hardly bear it. Progress has stalled almost completely. You start questioning the value and purpose of the project and consider abandoning it permanently: *Is a fence worth this much struggle?*

Now imagine the same scenario with a comfortable, peaceful home to return to. Recovery after hard work is now possible. The problem of energy management is eliminated, allowing you to focus completely on building that fence. Living in a subpar home means that significant effort is wasted on problems unrelated to your primary focus. Progress is possible, but it's exponentially more difficult.

This parallels why confidence and esteem are so important. Without them, much of your energy is consumed by more basic concerns unrelated to feature development. You feel inadequate and unskilled, and this means that you're more prone to quitting. When challenges arise, your inner critic builds on them, prompting self-sabotage. Stray negative thoughts are apt to land, grow, and take control, demanding you quit.

....

A strong foundation of confidence
and esteem not only makes life more
pleasant, but it's also critical for making
progress toward other goals.

....

FORTITUDE: ESTEEM AND CONFIDENCE

Before exploring further, let's parse the difference between esteem and confidence since each word is open to interpretation. In this book, self-esteem is how much you value yourself, while self-confidence is how much you believe in your abilities. While there is often overlap and influence between the two, the distinction can be important in certain circumstances.

When someone has high self-esteem, they value themselves highly, independent of external evaluations or comparisons. However, this doesn't automatically mean they're confident. They might say, for example: "I don't think I could ever be a musician. I just don't have the talent for it." At the same time, they may believe they're a worthwhile, valuable individual. Their sense of worth isn't impacted by belief (or non-belief) in their abilities.

The opposite is also possible: high-confidence and low self-esteem. These individuals believe in their abilities without valuing themselves. They might say, "I can make great music," but simultaneously feel worthless, unlovable, or like a bad person. Consider the wide number of famous musicians, athletes, and other performers with world-class talent but low self-worth. Many of these individuals develop substance abuse problems that serve to blanket their lack of self-esteem.

Struggles with confidence and/or esteem are common and inevitably limit happiness. We tend to either not try, quit quickly, or feel terrible, regardless of our actions. Your goal for this section is to explore how to develop both confidence and esteem. Moving forward, since many tactics build both traits in unison, I'll occasionally refer to them simultaneously using the term "fortitude" as shorthand. If one needs more attention than the other in your mindscape, adjust your focus accordingly.

GENERAL OR COMFORT CONFIDENCE?

Confidence can be further subdivided into general and comfort categories. Few of us are equally confident in all situations. Instead, we tend to be more confident in those areas where we have experience and expertise. We'll call this "comfort confidence." Most people have comfort confidence in at least a few categories.

Let's tunnel through how this works. Imagine a place where you're very confident—for example, at work. Here, your uncertainty is likely to be low. You usually know what actions to take, either from developing a skill set, knowing how to acquire help, or just through having experienced the environment many times. Certain events may be surprising or unpleasant, but you typically know how to act, and this creates confidence.

Contrast this with an unfamiliar activity or environment, perhaps the sport of fencing. It's likely that you have no experience to lean on, possess few or no associated skills, and may not even know how to find help. This increased uncertainty creates decreased confidence. *I'm not sure I'll ever understand this. I'm trying, but I'm not improving. Should I quit?"*

There's a dilemma. Confidence is most accessible in realms where you already have experience. But how can you gain the confidence to enter new situations? Fortunately, there's an answer. You can't gain comfort confidence in everything, but you can increase your certainty in your ability to handle uncertainty. This is where general confidence comes into play. General confidence is a belief in your ability to increase skill, apply experience, and utilize resources, even if the situation is currently difficult or uncomfortable.

General confidence is simply the confidence to navigate unfamiliar situations, even if imperfectly. It's not a lack of fear or unlimited bravado. It's not expecting immediate success whenever you try. It's not thinking *I could become a professional athlete, rock star musician, and groundbreaking scientist by next week.* It's accepting obstacles as they come, coping with uncomfortable emotions, and realizing they're an inevitable part of the process.

For example, say you accept a new project like learning guitar or buying an investment property. You don't need to believe you'll make a perfect album or buy the best margin home to have general confidence. You don't even need to believe you'll do the tasks well. You simply need to believe you're capable of picking up a guitar or contacting a realtor and working through the uncertainty, even if it's hard.

For most of us, developing general confidence is a painstaking process of developing new instances of comfort confidence in an intentional way. Each time you push through uncertainty, you become more accustomed to handling the process and, therefore, more generally confident. Consciously and intentionally moving through this process can be challenging, but it pays dividends.

Specifically, general confidence provides the mental resilience required to seize opportunities that lie beyond your comfort zone. These opportunities tend to produce sizable differences in your quality of life, such as changing careers for higher fulfillment and better pay. Those without general confidence tend to let those opportunities slip by year after year, too afraid to take action in the face of uncertainty.

Most importantly, general confidence provides the ability to weather life's inevitable, jarring, and unexpected changes. You may be comfortable now, but what if you lose your job or are forced to move? If you lack belief in your ability to manage uncertainty, it will be an extremely unpleasant, stressful experience. General confidence won't make change pleasant, but it will be an order of magnitude more manageable than it would be otherwise.

Here's a question you can use to gauge your general confidence level: If you had to move to a new country, change occupations, leave loved ones, and start a new life, how confident are you that you could eventually build an enjoyable life? This is an extreme example, but it gets to the heart of handling massive uncertainty. The strength of belief in your ability to handle uncertainty also hints at your likelihood of taking the corresponding action, whether by choice or due to circumstance.

Thinking in terms of homebuilding, general confidence is like the structure of your home, while comfort confidences are individual rooms. Having lots of rooms doesn't necessarily improve your home's quality or structure. A solid structure, however, makes it far easier to add future rooms. Additional rooms are nice, but your real goal is to build a solid foundation.

As we explore homebuilding tactics, look for ways to channel existing comfort confidence into general confidence. You may uncover tactics that show how you've overcome uncertainty in the past. These same tactics can be useful during future uncertain situations, providing flexibility and resilience. We won't specifically hone in on this topic again, but it's worth considering as you move through the exercises later.

COMPLETING A HOME INSPECTION

After your landscape survey, it should be no surprise that home inspections are also useful. Knowing your home's composition, structural integrity, and history allows you to make wise decisions about future projects. Otherwise, you may run into familiar problems, haphazardly tackling whatever happens to catch your attention. In homebuilding, this manifests as working on the wrong rooms and neglecting the foundation.

Home inspections are essentially a subgroup within landscape surveys. Both processes are identical, heavily utilizing tunneling. The primary difference is that home inspections focus exclusively on tunneling around fortitude without including accomplishments, solutions, and values: How do I feel about myself? How confident am I in my abilities? How often do I act, even when I'm uncertain?

As you tunnel through these questions, you're likely to encounter thoughts like *I'll never be able to find love.* During home inspections, you should prioritize discovering the origin of these thoughts over finding solutions. Why do you feel unlovable? A particularly difficult break-up? Comments from others? Lack of experience? Your current goal is understanding how your esteem and confidence are composed. The solutions will come later.

Here are a few starter questions to tunnel through:

- ➜ How do you feel about yourself?
- ➜ What do you think you're capable of accomplishing?
- ➜ Do you feel like you deserve happiness?
- ➜ How capable are you of achieving your goals?
- ➜ How well would you handle a major life change?
- ➜ How often do you undertake new challenges?

These feed into the two primary questions:

- ➜ Do you value yourself?
- ➜ Do you believe you can successfully navigate new situations?

Tunneling through these questions can be harder than expected, as reflecting on fortitude tends to bring sensitive personal topics to the surface. For this reason, you might find it helps to imagine the process as a dialogue between two roles. One side asks questions to deeply understand your position, while also being staunchly supportive of your worth and abilities. The other side answers as your most honest and authentic self. Writing this faux exchange can especially help in producing clarity. It may feel strange at first, but this method helps depersonalize the content, making unbiased and realistic reflection easier.

Dedicated reflection times can be supplemented with in-the-moment evaluations. One tactic for producing real-time data is setting random timers throughout the day. When these timers go off, note your thoughts and feelings around your confidence and esteem at that moment. Done often enough, for long enough, you'll start to become more aware of your feelings of fortitude in any given situation, and patterns will emerge around the situations that need strengthening the most.

There are other ways to enact a home inspection; the above are just example tactics for illustration purposes. You can also co-opt tactics from the self-survey section and mold them around fortitude to produce insights. The important part is finding a method for understanding your confidence and esteem in a range of different circumstances.

CLEARING THE GROUND

Building fortitude requires a belief along the lines of *I am inherently valuable and capable of increasing happiness.* For most, this will seem reasonable. Some, however, have powerful, negative thought habits built from past experiences. While unraveling these patterns typically takes time and effort, we'll explore a few high-level arguments against common beliefs that lower fortitude.

One common debilitating belief is feeling that you don't deserve happiness. This often stems from a belief that you are unworthy or unimportant. My first question is: What system is this judgment being derived from? The answer typically mentions one or more of the following: family, religion, or societal expectations. Besides exposing happiness to external control, how accurate is that perception? What do these individuals or systems gain by restricting your optimization of happiness?

Your family may be concerned about your value hierarchy and choices, but they generally don't want you to be unhappy. All mainstream religions preach of fulfilling a greater purpose, which is the top of your happiness hierarchy. The expectations of society are vague, location-dependent, and often based more on personal perception than fact. There may be some external pressure against the ways you currently derive happiness, but that doesn't at all imply you don't deserve it.

There are other reasons individuals hold this belief, but the foundations are always fragile or needlessly self-imposed. No one benefits from your lack of fortitude. Anyone that says otherwise, including yourself, is looking from a skewed perspective. Everyone deserves happiness, regardless of who they are or what they've done.

If it helps, imagine holding a diamond covered in mud. Would you say, "There's mud here, what's in my hand has no value"? Of course not, yet many of us treat ourselves this way, allowing mistakes and life problems to permanently destroy our personal value. Individual worth is always there, whether or not you choose to look past the mud on the surface.

Another common belief is that *nothing matters in the infinite scale of time and the universe.* At the very least, you must live through experiences. If nothing matters objectively, then you're free to make any choice. Given all choices are equal, more desirable experiences are preferable. The universe doesn't need inherent rules to make optimizing happiness worthwhile; you just need to exist and, consequently, have experience. This may mean nothing ten billion years from now, but if you believe nothing matters, then that doesn't matter either.

The belief that happiness is fixed also comes up occasionally. This is easy to disprove. Start by comparing outcomes of varying desirability, then consider your influence on contributing factors. Consider something as simple as being thirsty. You can choose to drink water or wait and become further dehydrated. If happiness was fixed, you'd expect to feel the same either way, which isn't the case.

Perhaps explicitly considering the opposite is easier. If happiness is fixed, you shouldn't be able to make yourself miserable either. If I asked you to make yourself less happy, however, you could certainly do it. No one would argue whether it's possible. If choices can make life worse, then they can make life better as well.

....

Most strong, repetitive feelings of worthlessness are rooted in habit or trauma rather than rationality. Breaking these patterns typically takes time and practice.

....

SELF-FULFILLING BELIEFS

What you believe largely determines what you do. Accordingly, believing in your ability to create happiness is critical. Your frames dictate your perceived options and subsequent actions. If you don't see an option as possible, then you won't take action, effectively making it impossible.

Imagine creating your own board game. If you implement a rule that moving two spaces is impossible, you'll never move two spaces. Physical reality says it's possible to move a piece two spaces, but your self-chosen rules dictate that you never will. It's your game, though. You can change the rules whenever you want. While it may not always feel like it, perceptions of possibilities work in much the same way.

Your options aren't based on objective truth, but on the perspective you take and the paths you see. When you explore your perceptions, you begin to see new options. *The rule says I can't move two spaces—why? Maybe it would be better without that rule, even though that's how I've always done it.* Without this process, default perceptions rule our lives, often for the worse.

Here's an example to illustrate the power of default perceptions. Let's say you have a co-worker. On your first day of work, they don't welcome you and give you a snide look. You know they dislike you. Any time they offer kindness now, it feels fake. You can tell it's a ruse. They're just waiting for the right moment to strike, ruining you however they can.

That's all well and good, but what if your feeling of *knowing* is a strong but misguided perception? What if they genuinely like you but had a bad day? Now, there's nothing they can do to change your mind. Your frame will always trump their actions. Any action can be justified under "I know they don't like me." This shows the power of unquestioned perceptions. Regardless of how true they are, perceptions control your experience. But you can control your perceptions. How does this concept apply to happiness? The belief you can create happiness is essential. Without it, you'll feel powerless to challenge the negative frames that shape how you evaluate experiences. When negative thoughts attack your esteem and confidence, they threaten to overpower even the most desirable states. Life is hard enough without constant self-flagellation.

Consider the most negative person you know. Someone who constantly verbalizes inadequacy, the futility of effort, and fear of failure. How happy would you say they are? How much do they enjoy life, even in the best circumstances? Are they at their full potential? Most of these individuals don't believe better results are possible, so they don't take action. A lack of action guarantees no results.

You might be asking: "What about those who constantly talk without accomplishing anything? My friend reads all sorts of self-help content and is still miserable and unsuccessful." Belief alone doesn't guarantee anything. It must be combined with action. We'll discuss the specifics of consistently taking action later. The point here is that without belief, you're practically guaranteed inaction and lack of progress.

HOMEBUILDING AS A PROCESS

Even when you understand and accept all the previous assertions, your lifelong habitual frames won't dissolve overnight. As with building a home, increasing your fortitude takes time. It's a gradual process of identifying, removing, and replacing disempowering thoughts with more desirable patterns, so pick your projects wisely.

If you remodeled an actual home with no experience, it would be ambitious, and perhaps even foolish to rebuild it all at once. Picking one or two smaller sub-projects is far more manageable. Replace the carpet, then upgrade the electrical work later. It makes sense to strategize building fortitude similarly. As you explore tactics, extract the one or two areas that need the most work and focus there.

With each successful home remodel, you will add tools, skills, and knowledge to your repertoire for use in future projects. Subsequent projects become easier as you gain experience with the process. Similarly, as you recondition your thoughts to support fortitude, the process becomes faster and easier. Over time, you'll be able to build simultaneously across more realms and with less effort.

Unfortunately, the first few projects, when you're most vulnerable, are usually the most arduous. It may take multiple attempts, but you need to keep pushing back against disempowering thoughts, like *This is stupid, there's no point. You're either confident or not. I'll never be good enough.* With time and effort, these thoughts will eventually weaken in frequency and intensity, while you will also become more adept at handling them. To achieve this, you only need to tackle one sub-project at a time.

TACTICS FOR BUILDING FORTITUDE

You're now ready to explore tactics for homebuilding. As with previous sections, these exercises are generally effective but should be piloted individually for efficacy. The results won't be the same for everyone, but most people should be able to extract something useful. If not, I recommend exploring additional resources for building confidence and esteem. As always, it's more important to build fortitude than it is to use any particular exercise.

CHALLENGE NEGATIVE THOUGHTS

Due to the nature of the mind, negative thoughts can never be completely eliminated. In many cases, they serve a useful purpose, helping gauge the desirability of different states. Generally, however, they overreach their usefulness and cause undesirable outcomes. Accordingly, developing tools for quickly and efficiently managing negative thoughts will always be useful. The tool we'll focus on here is how to see thoughts more realistically, then challenge and dissolve them.

Here's an example: You're considering applying for a promotion when a thought arises. *I'll never get promoted. I don't deserve it. I don't have the experience or skill.* You obviously want the job, but your thought habits are undermining that desire. There's a fortitude gap. If you're lucky enough to notice the thought, you can tunnel into it, challenging your frames along the way.

—*Why do you think you can't or shouldn't be promoted?*

—*I don't deserve it, everyone else is more qualified.*

—What does it mean to deserve a promotion? How can you become more qualified? What can you learn by trying, even if you don't get it?

Rather than deal with more examples of negative thoughts, let's shift focus to two approaches for challenging disempowering thoughts: position reversal and relevant action steps.

In position reversal, you consider the opposite of your original thought using equally strong arguments. This creates a more realistic assessment of the situation and shows how polarized your original thought was. For example, the thought *I don't deserve a promotion* might be challenged with *Why do I deserve a promotion?* Stay with the thought until you find at least one positive answer.

The mind is exceptionally good at rationalizing any given position. Once your focus has shifted, multiple justifications will typically come to mind. This alone may not change your mind, but it at least reveals the situation as less one-sided than it seemed, thus weakening disempowering thoughts.

You might also challenge the thought: *you'll never get promoted* with its opposite: *You'll always get promoted.* The goal isn't genuinely believing the second position, but realizing both positions are equally unreasonable. As with most uncertain events, promotions only happen sometimes. For a chance at success, however, you must make an attempt. Seeing both positions simultaneously helps move evaluations away from extremism toward functional realism.

You can also challenge debilitating thoughts with actionable solutions. Questions starting with "How can I...?" are extremely effective at focusing on the next tangible steps. For example, "How can I become the most qualified individual for the job?" naturally leads to thinking about relevant action steps. Using "How can I..." questions shifts your focus away from self-judgment and toward solutions.

The hardest part of this tactic is noticing negative thoughts and then remembering to challenge them, as there's usually too much noise to keep track of thoughts throughout the day. Instead, pick a scenario or event where debilitating thoughts are common and focus your attention there. You'll get far more opportunities to practice. For example, say you usually feel negative, nervous, or low-worth during sports. Setting a reminder of your intention to challenge negative thoughts before games is more likely to produce results than trying to catch everything throughout the day.

Here's what that example might look like. Before a baseball game, you have the thought: *I'm going to challenge negative thoughts as I play today.* During the game, you catch yourself thinking *I'll never hit the ball. This pitcher is too good.* You can then introduce extreme position reversal or relevant action steps. *"I'll always hit every pitch. This pitcher is the worst. Alright, that seems like a stretch."* or *"What evidence do I have that I can hit against good pitchers? There was that game a few weeks ago..."* or *"How can I adjust my swing to hit the next ball? How can I predict the pitch?"*

Ideally, these challenges will bring you to a more realistic, focused place where you can both feel and perform better.

When this works, missing becomes less important. It's no longer a good basis for self-sabotage or quitting. You still have reason to believe you can hit the next pitch. You can keep looking for actions to improve the next outcome. Getting used to this way of thinking takes time, but it encourages continuous effort in spite of difficulty or emotional duress. This trait, otherwise called resilience, is critical for success in most long-term projects. The difference between success and failure is often just down to the number of attempts made.

....

Persevering is far easier when you're equipped to handle the thoughts trying to hold you back.

....

TACKLE UNCERTAINTY

How often do you intentionally expose yourself to uncomfortable or uncertain situations? For most, the answer is never. Discomfort is unpleasant, so we're wired to avoid it. Yet, the intensity of distress we feel during uncertainty is proportional to the experience we have at managing discomfort. By intentionally increasing your exposure, you create opportunities to build familiarity with, and tools for, dealing with discomfort. While unpleasant by its very nature, pushing through discomfort allows you to increase resilience in a controlled manner and on your own terms.

Intentionally tackling uncertainty may sound unnecessary, but consider the stories of growth born from struggle. It's common to hear individuals talk about moving countries, switching careers, or living through other highly uncertain events as enlightening and crucial to their growth. Living through these events creates feelings of vulnerability, uncertainty, and discomfort. To survive new environments, we need to push through discomfort and adapt. The more practice you have with withstanding uncertainty, the more experience you have to draw from in future situations.

Change countries? Just to experience adversity? That's a bit overkill, don't you think? No, thanks. Don't worry, I'm not asking you to undertake a serious life-altering change unless you want to. The examples are simply here to illustrate how uncertainty facilitates growth in fortitude. This is equally true whether done by choice or circumstance. When you choose to become familiar with and overcome discomfort, on your own terms, you will find it easier to manage the instances where life thrusts it upon you.

Here's an example of how you might intentionally tackle discomfort. Let's say your blueprint includes expanding your social circle. Talking to new people makes you uncomfortable because face-to-face interpersonal reactions are uncertain and intense. There are ways to build a social circle without starting conversations with strangers, but if you want to build fortitude, you might choose to start conversations with strangers precisely because it does make you feel uncomfortable.

Let's say you start attending networking events. The first event is likely to feel extremely uncomfortable as you have no experience to draw from. The event doesn't go as planned. You only have two conversations when your goal is ten. To make matters worse, both conversations felt awkward. You feel even more uncomfortable than before. At this point, you might be ready to give up, but you've just hit the point where meaningful work can be done.

A primary intention in attending the event was creating and working through this very discomfort—time to start tunneling. You can now intentionally lean into the feeling and experience of discomfort, recognizing its quality and identifying ways to adapt. Pay close attention to the quality of your self-talk, as it often deteriorates with discomfort. This process is by no means easy, but each experience becomes slightly easier as you become accustomed to accepting and managing the feeling.

Each subsequent event will likely be less uncomfortable. This is through a combination of gaining experience with both the type of event and managing discomfort. The intent of facing uncertainty isn't to eliminate discomfort. It's to determine which tools allow you to thrive in, or at least tolerate, uncomfortable situations.

At some point, you will have gained so much comfort confidence that networking events become less useful for building general confidence. To continue increasing your skill in handling discomfort, you must continue to experience challenging levels of discomfort, which involves tackling entirely different uncomfortable tasks. This is how you can develop a toolset for managing uncertainty across many situations, whether intentional or externally imposed.

Framing is critically important to this tactic. It must be clear from the outset why you're experiencing discomfort. Remember, the goal is feeling discomfort so you can manage it better. Resist the temptation to avoid it altogether. Failing to develop this toolset leaves you vulnerable to mandatory discomfort. Better to build the skills on your terms than wait for life to force you into experiences you're ill-equipped to handle.

ACCEPT CHALLENGES

Another way to increase fortitude is by taking on challenges. Completing challenges creates accomplishments, improves skills, and provides evidence of your discipline and capabilities. By expanding your list of accomplishments, you become more likely to remember difficulties you've already overcome, increasing your overall confidence.

Taking on challenges may sound similar to facing uncertainty, and there can be overlap, but they're not equivalent. Challenges must be difficult, but they don't necessarily need to involve uncertainty. For example, writing 3,000 words every day for a year is difficult but not uncertain. You already know how to write words. The challenging part is writing that many words consistently. This tactic creates opportunities to become more comfortable with the discomfort of difficulty, as opposed to uncertainty. As a bonus, undertaking challenges tends to develop valuable skills and attributes.

An ideal challenge has a few attributes. The first is that it actually requires pushing into difficult terrain. Fear of failure tends to constrain challenges to tasks well within your comfort zone, practically guaranteeing success. While you may avoid feeling uncomfortable, you also miss opportunities to increase your confidence by managing discomfort.

There's debate about just how audacious challenges should be, but aiming beyond comfort is the bare minimum for increasing fortitude. This varies by case and individual. Running one mile a day is plenty challenging for the average person, but probably won't push a marathon runner. You don't need to write five novels this year or travel around the world with no money to experience difficulty. You just need to make an effort to accomplish a task beyond your current grasp. Sometimes that requires large leaps, other times small increments.

This leads to the next point. Challenges are most likely to be successful when backed by genuine commitment. This means tying them to blueprint components and being able to articulate at least one emotionally compelling reason for undertaking the challenge, beyond knowing its use in homebuilding. During especially trying moments, you can lean on these reasons for motivation. Difficulty can be uncomfortable, but there are good reasons for facing it directly.

If implementing this tactic seems vague, it's because the next major section is dedicated to following through on your goals. For now, brainstorm some challenges you can commit to, including how they relate to your blueprint. You can flesh out the details later, after reading about the implementation specifics.

SHARE YOUR EXPERTISE

Sharing expertise is another useful tactic for increasing fortitude. To start, you must develop, stay current with, and expand your skills and knowledge in a realm. This tends to produce comfort confidence. In addition, teaching transmits skills and knowledge to others, which most people find valuable. Directly seeing interpersonal, positive impact arising from your efforts often leads to greater self-worth and esteem. Finally, sharing expertise frequently raises unfamiliar questions, providing opportunities to manage uncertainty.

Sharing expertise first requires that you develop it. This is easier than it seems. Many individuals believe only world-class experts with extensive experience and accomplishment should share their expertise. That's an incredibly high standard, which few accomplish. Expertise can be shared long before attaining mastery.

I'm glad you let anyone teach anything, but I want my information from the best, most-qualified experts. This position fails to recognize an important point. The necessary level of domain-specific knowledge depends entirely on the student and the desired outcome. Did a world-class professional teach you how to drive? Should six-year-old soccer players only be coached by Premier League athletes? Of course not. Their experience level dictates a need for the fundamentals. Many individuals are capable of teaching these lower-level skills.

In fact, reaching for world-class experts, especially those who don't regularly teach, too early can cause unexpected obstacles. Most experts learned the fundamentals, and possibly even advanced skills, many years ago. It's habitually integrated into their actions. Over time, they may have lost familiarity with the types of problems beginners face, making it hard to compose useful tactics. If experts don't choose to hone the skill of teaching, they can lose touch with those just starting out.

This means that it's usually more effective to learn from individuals with amateur or intermediate expertise. Individuals with this level of expertise have more recently solved the same problems beginners often face. You don't need to be the best, you just need to have slightly more or different skills than the person you're teaching. Returning to the soccer example, one player's general skills might be sub-par, but they may have an incredible shot. Another player whose skills are generally better could still benefit from learning the first player's shooting technique.

This is also true for individuals of roughly equal skill. For example, two experienced cooks can share new recipes that expand each other's knowledge. By collaborating, they create the opportunity to learn new skills and techniques. This is often how high-skill individuals refine and perfect their craft over time, combining their unique history with information learned from others.

The point is you already have, or can quickly develop, expertise worth sharing. Consider your strengths, realms where you have experience or talent, and your achievements. What do others say you're good at? How can you help others expand their knowledge or skills? What have you recently overcome? You don't have to be world-class to help bridge the gap.

After settling on an expertise, determine how you'll share information. Do you want to write articles, make videos, or attend meet-ups? Do you want to teach beginners or interact with peers? Formally or informally? Online or offline? There are no wrong answers, just options based on your comfort level and interest. This tactic has many potential benefits, so it's worth a try.

TRACK AND REVIEW ACCOMPLISHMENTS

Sometimes we need a reminder of what we've already done to feel empowered. Reviewing your accomplishments provides historical evidence that you've overcome discomfort, uncertainty, and difficulty before. Looking through these events reminds you of your capacity for completing goals. It also allows you to celebrate and feel proud of what you've done, which may be neglected by a "what's next?" attitude. When challenging situations arise, you're more likely to remember these examples and use them to keep pushing onward or combat negative thoughts.

This tactic is fairly easy to complete if you've previously explored your strengths. Start by listing accomplishments that took the most effort. Effort is preferable to overall outcomes because you're looking for proof that effort impacts results. Low-effort accomplishments don't prove resilience. Remembering your natural gift for math won't convince you to push through when writing proves difficult. On the other hand, remembering the long hours you spent studying for a degree might help convince you to keep working through your relationship problems.

Reviewing accomplishments should also elicit feelings of resilience, motivation, and pride. Events that didn't require a growth of fortitude are unlikely to be helpful during difficult moments. They may come to mind, but with little impact on your emotional state and associated frames. While still potentially useful, achievements associated with positive emotions are generally more effective than those which are purely logical.

Let's explore a concrete example of the implications here. Practically everyone would include a college degree on their resume. It's a notable, socially recognized achievement. The majority of graduates worked hard and feel pride in their accomplishments. Let's say one individual earned their degree while supporting a family, working multiple jobs, and studying countless long nights. Knowing the difficulties they faced, how effort impacted their results, and the positive feelings associated with the achievement makes it a perfect accomplishment to reflect on.

Another individual may not find the same accomplishment meaningful at all. They went to college on a scholarship, hardly tried, and cheated substantially. For them, the achievement proves nothing about difficulty or effort but instead produces feelings of guilt. Revisiting this process is pointless. From the outside, these accomplishments are equally noteworthy. From the inside, however, how each individual relates to the accomplishment determines how useful they are in building fortitude.

This means any achievement is worth reflecting on if it reminds you of your abilities, regardless of outcomes relative to others. Imagine seeing two people walking down the sidewalk. One is a completely average individual. The other shattered both legs and spent five years rebuilding their strength to walk again. The outcomes are equal, but you naturally give much larger credence to the second person's resilience. Extend the same kindness to yourself by considering your journey holistically when choosing which achievements you'll review.

After creating a list, set aside time each day to reflect on those accomplishments. Five minutes a day or so is plenty. During these reflections, focus on the process, more than the achievement itself. How did you stay motivated? What did you feel, and how did you handle it? How did you keep making progress? This will familiarize you not just with results but the process of resilience in the face of difficulty. When those moments arise, you'll be far more prepared to handle them, helped by the tools you've already used for success.

You could also start an accomplishment journal. During each reflection session, simply write down one recent action that required real effort from you. This creates a granular record of your steps toward your goal, which hones your focus on the process. When you hit a milestone, you'll have a detailed account of all the steps it took to get there.

You can also use this journal for reflection, flipping to a random page, or during especially challenging times. You'll see the specific details of how you made progress in the past, proving what you're capable of. Saturate your mind with this information. Eventually, it will be what comes to mind as you consider taking on new challenges, thus increasing your confidence in your ability to achieve.

VISUALIZATION

Visualizations can be a good way to build confidence. By imagining a future event in vivid detail, you generate a rough familiarity with the experience. You can preemptively consider roadblocks and devise solutions, increasing flexibility when the event arrives. You can't, however, predict experiences with full fidelity. That means visualization isn't a replacement for action, but a supplement.

Visualization is a simple concept, but it's hard to utilize effectively. Intuitive visualizations are typically high-level, lacking detail and depth. The closer you are to mentally replicating the event, however, the more useful your pseudo-experience becomes. It takes practice to imagine scenarios in a form where you can fully explore how you might react to particular events.

Let's walk through the example of visualizing smoother conversations with a difficult co-worker. First, find a quiet place to relax and focus. Then, close your eyes and imagine the situation. You might begin by visualizing walking over to your co-worker. Then imagine the greeting you'll use, how you feel, and how they might respond. Focus on specific dialog, facial expressions, gestures, etc. More detail is generally better.

You may also want to repeat the scene multiple times with slight variations. This means covering several possible reactions from your co-worker. Creating one perfect recitation isn't the best approach, because the real event won't occur exactly as imagined. Working through different scenarios creates flexibility, thus increasing your confidence in your ability to adapt. The actual event will be different, but the more options you've considered, the more prepared you'll be.

Useful visualizations have desirable outcomes, but that doesn't mean the scenario must develop perfectly. For example, an athlete might imagine taking the game-winning shot unhindered. Then they might imagine making the shot again while being fouled. The second scenario isn't perfect, but it's plausible. Walking through a range of potential events prepares you to course-correct, even if events don't unfold exactly as planned. This generally translates to less uncertainty and increased confidence.

Visualization can also be used to increase performance and follow-through, making it overlap with concepts in the section on landscaping. For the sake of keeping all visualization-related information in one place, I'll share a few examples of how it can be used for implementation and productivity.

Visualization of Daily Schedule

One common visualization, especially useful for those working on time management, is exploring an idealized upcoming day. For example, I'd imagine my workout, shower, breakfast, traveling to work, contributing to projects, meetings, returning home, editing this book, sleeping, and everything in between.

This covers a lot of ground so, unlike visualizations for confidence, don't worry if the intimate details are more muted. At important points of the day, however, slow down and increase the granularity. For example, working on this book is important to me. A visualization of this part of my day might include how it feels to hit my daily goal, how long it takes, and how clear my thoughts and focus are. I could increase the granularity by imagining how sitting at my desk feels, the room temperature, and the sensation of pushing keys. This can be done several times over until the process of enacting the important task feels clear and crisp.

When working on the book later, these images will be vivid and recent. I naturally know which actions align with my visualization because I've solidified an agenda for the day. Less ambiguity between tasks means less opportunity to get distracted and more follow-through. This doesn't guarantee action or perfection, but you might be surprised by how effective this tactic is. A clear mental model of the day makes actualization much easier.

Visualization of New Habits

Visualization can also help in creating new habits. By imagining making the preferred decision at difficult points, you can be prepared for when the event arrives. You can anticipate your feelings and plan for challenges or potential complications when making the decision. Seeing and feeling the preferred choice beforehand also removes the friction of deciding in the moment, when temptations are stronger.

For example, I've used this tactic for diet change. Each morning, I imagined what I would eat, when, and how it would make me feel. I also explored scenarios with temptations of unhealthy treats or the urge to overeat. Then I imagined how I would feel after each choice. This helped me stick to the plan, discover weak points, and remember the long-term consequences of my actions.

This style of visualization is especially useful for deeply ingrained habits. It focuses your awareness on each relevant decision, mentally highlighting important choices. This increased awareness makes choosing the desired behavior more likely, instead of mindlessly reverting to your default. Again, it's not a guarantee of action, but a nudge in the right direction.

Visualization of Important Events

Finally, visualization can be useful for important one-off, high-stress, or infrequent events. It's typically impossible to gain direct experience of this kind of event, as they don't happen often. So, in some cases, visualization is one of the only viable options for preparation.

For example, let's say your company has suddenly been involved in a scandal. They've booked you for an interview with a reporter in one hour. The interview will be broadcast live to millions of people. None of the questions have been shared with you beforehand. There's no time to practice mock interviews.

The best you can do is rehearse your answers to expected questions, verbally or mentally. Visualizing the situation from start to finish provides one method for practice when you're otherwise highly constrained. This example may seem somewhat contrived, but many situations don't allow for direct experience beforehand, and it's at least useful to consider how you might act before the event. It's not ideal, but it's better than nothing.

Visualization isn't a cure-all, but it is a flexible tool for your arsenal. While not a replacement for direct experience, it's definitely a useful supplement to action and can fill gaps when the direct experience isn't available. It's worth experimenting with a few different styles to gauge how and when visualization can be of use in your mindscape.

POSITIVE AFFIRMATIONS

Affirmations have a mixed reputation for effectiveness. When used properly, however, they can be a powerful tool for increasing fortitude. If you're unfamiliar with the term, affirmations are simply words or phrases that you repeat regularly. While repetition may seem mundane, it paves neural pathways, making particular ideas surface more readily. Over time, this shifts your default focus to more empowering, useful thoughts.

Like many skeptics, I tried affirmations and thought they were pointless. I spent one full year reciting an affirmation akin to "I am a king among men. Success flows to me." Some obscure sources claimed daily recitation would increase fortitude. Month after month passed with no tangible difference in my daily experience. I dismissed the tactic as bunk.

Later, I realized the affirmation was ineffective because it lacked personal meaning and focused externally, making comparisons with others. The phrase came to mind often but held no logical or emotional weight. Accordingly, it had no impact on my behavior.

Consider the affirmation, "I am a pickle." No amount of repetition will make you believe that's true (I hope...). Reciting a meaningless statement does little to alter your beliefs or behavior, it simply brings certain ideas to mind more readily. If you said, "I am a pickle" every day for five years, even if not believing it literally, it might be your first thought in response to "What are you?" It wouldn't, however, convince you that you were a pickle.

The intention of using affirmations is to burn phrases into your brain so they arise during relevant choices. Their presence is a necessary precursor in using them to guide decisions. To be effective, however, they must also be meaningful, controllable, and aligned with your beliefs. In most cases, this means writing them yourself.

Creating personal affirmations, however, is harder than borrowing them. I've included a few examples to help. You're not meant to use these examples, but I hope they give you some ideas while brainstorming your own.

- → I have confidence in my ability to adapt and be successful.
- → I accept myself and feel in control of my life.

➜ I am good enough to accomplish my dreams.

➜ I am worthy of unconditional love, including from myself.

➜ I am capable of accomplishing any task I set my mind to.

After creating your affirmation(s), double-check they mirror your beliefs, are meaningful, and controllable. Then decide how often to recite them. As a guideline, anything less than once a day is unlikely to be effective. A standard method is to recite affirmations shortly after waking up, setting the day's tone. Verbal recitations are common, but they can be read or recorded and listened to as well. The details are flexible. Experiment to see what feels right to you.

You can make affirmations even more memorable by adding visual cues to your environment. For example, I usually keep a whiteboard with affirmations in both my bedroom and office. Other common places are bathroom mirrors, car windshields, and computer or phone screensavers. Again, you're simply repeating these messages, so they're likely to come to mind during relevant choices.

This is the same process that's used by motivational posters and other items. They increase the frequency of a particular message. If the message resonates with you, you're more likely to remember it and act that way. If you're indifferent, the message still comes to mind more easily, but you may not act on it. Recent, repeated information is more available and more likely to influence your choices.

By the same token, you may consider curating the content you consume most often. For example, constantly seeking stories or news of violence skews your perception of its frequency. The same can be said of information on almost any subject. There is a place and purpose for unpleasant information, but mindless, constant consumption has a way of erecting barriers to happiness. It's worth reflecting on the quality of the content that you spend the most time with.

One last note, we focused on affirmations for building fortitude, but they can also be used to reinforce habits, goals, and values. Any idea can be made more available by increasing the frequency of exposure, making it more likely to become an action. That won't automatically align every thought, action, and feeling with optimized happiness, but it's a useful tool for nudging you in the right direction.

CONTRACTORS: OUTSIDE INFLUENCES ON FORTITUDE

We've covered a number of options for increasing fortitude from a solitary position, but rarely is life so isolated. While you ultimately hold responsibility for fortitude, growth is impacted by your social interactions. Accordingly, it's worth spending some time considering the implications of who you spend time with and how you think about their actions.

DIVORCING FEELINGS FROM EXTERNAL ACTIONS

Each social interaction is the equivalent of allowing a contractor into your home. The power you relinquish, dictated by how much you internalize external actions, determines their impact. You can control whether these contractors can make adjustments, whether they're trying to build or destroy your home. Social influences on fortitude are exclusively based on what you accept, which is a matter of framing.

This can be difficult to digest. *How am I at fault when my brother calls me a failure?* I want to be clear: the way others treat you is not your fault. You can, however, control whether you accept and internalize those actions. By learning to divorce your worth and confidence from others' actions, you increase control over the homebuilding process. You choose which contractors have power in your home.

Think of it like this; if a contractor said, "We should knock out the wall of your bedroom and expose it to the elements." Would you do it? Of course not. You'd recognize it's a destructive, pointless blueprint for your home. Now consider being called stupid. This blueprint is equally unproductive. Why would you choose to entertain and enhance the idea?

Here's another way to look at it. Any statement from another person is purely perspective, which may or may not be true. Imagine I say, "you seem like a dinosaur." No matter how much I believe it and how often or how forcefully I say it, it's just an opinion. My belief doesn't dictate reality. You don't have to believe it just because I do.

So why does being called a dinosaur have less impact than being called "a failure"? It can't be external factors, because they're equally subjective. Neither statement can be proven objectively true. The only difference is being a failure is a thought most of us consider identifying with. But you don't have to. You can intervene in the process.

To practice, pinpoint times when an external comment or action influenced your feelings of fortitude. Then tunnel through a few questions. What frame did I choose for this event? How am I coloring my interpretation with my own fears and perceptions? Am I internalizing an external opinion?

The answers can create drastically different internal experiences for external events. Consider being told, "Chew with your mouth closed; you're disgusting." This can be internalized as *I am disgusting*. With tunneling, however, you might frame it as "This person prefers I chew with my mouth closed." External opinions say more about another person's experience than they do about you. Your self-evaluations need not include those experiences.

I recognize dismantling demeaning comments and actions can be difficult, especially when they're frequent and/or come from those you admire or respect. These cases, unfortunately, are all too common. Even in the best case, where everyone around you has good intent, external events will attempt to influence your fortitude. Building this skill allows you to optimize the positive and minimize the negative.

If it helps, consider every action from others as a contractor presenting a blueprint for your home. Enacting these blueprints is always optional. Whether they're helpful, misguided, ill-intentioned, or confused, you are always the chief architect. Act like you would with a real home: keep what's useful and discard the rest.

MANAGING BAD CONTRACTORS

Handling bad contractors is an inevitable part of life. However, not all contractors are equally bad. Is it a one-off comment or a constant stream of abuse? The solution varies drastically by context. In this section, we'll cover common bad contractors and how to manage those relationships.

We'll start with simple one-off situations, like being called "cheap" by a store clerk. Here, you don't care about the relationship and gain nothing by feeding the situation. The solution is to either leave or ignore the comment. Further interaction is pointless, even to defend or explain yourself. Would you try to disprove "you seem like a dinosaur"? If you've divorced your feelings from the situation, you should be able to walk away without concern.

Managing single instances of bad contracting is fairly straightforward. It's mostly about getting space from the situation. Our most frequent associations tend to be more complicated. Most relationships create some value, even if they also produce negative forces against esteem. Leaving the relationship entirely is a difficult choice with noticeable consequences. In this case, your options are to reshape, limit, or remove these relationships, in that order.

Reshaping is the ideal tactic but requires enough goodwill for a straightforward conversation and commitment from both sides. In reshaping, you explain the impact of particular behaviors while asking for reasons why they are acting that way. The actions you find frustrating may be accidental, unknown, or incomplete. Motivations must be understood before asking for a change. Otherwise, it's too easy to make incorrect assumptions about how to reshape interactions effectively.

For example, say your significant other constantly dismisses your ideas about travel: "I don't think that's a good idea." You feel unsupported and constrained. Your first thought might be to push back harder: "I'm frustrated. Stop shooting down my dreams. If we don't go on a trip this year, I'm leaving you!" More pressure might achieve the intended outcome, but at the cost of goodwill in the relationship.

Instead of pushing back, imagine explaining your position and asking why your partner is acting that way. Perhaps you discover they didn't realize how seriously you wanted to travel. Or maybe their highest priority is saving for a home. At no point was the intent to shoot down your aspirations. Instead, they expected to spend money differently. They weren't intentionally creating negative blueprints; a communication gap was negatively coloring both of your frames. With increased mutual understanding, you can now cooperatively negotiate a path forward. Those who truly care about you are rarely intentionally bad contractors.

This doesn't work for all relationships. Some individuals actually don't care. Others don't have the discipline, understanding, or desire to change. Some are committed to ineffective tactics or values. If your attempts at reshaping don't work, the next option is limiting the relationship. This can apply to the relationship as a whole or just in specific contexts, depending on the situation.

Many people in our lives aren't solely good or bad contractors. Instead, their quality depends on the surrounding circumstances. In most circumstances, you can limit these relationships to avoid negative interactions. For example, perhaps conversations with your parents about career goals always lead to scorn and frustration. If reshaping hasn't helped, bypassing these conversations is often a better option.

A small percentage of individuals really are just bad contractors. They actively try to undermine fortitude or don't care about your feelings at all. Social context can make it challenging to remove these individuals from our lives. For example, if they're coworkers or a family member's significant other. In these circumstances, you can limit the relationship. You can also prepare for necessary interactions accordingly, knowing negative blueprints are likely to arise. Simply deciding to ignore negative comments goes a long way in maintaining composure.

Unfortunately, there are cases where limiting isn't enough. As behavior slides from negativity into verbal abuse and threats, the only option becomes removing the person from your life. Extracting yourself from such a situation may not be easy, but the decision should be. Anyone treating you with violent animosity will perpetually undermine happiness and potentially even your safety. The cost of continued interaction is almost certainly higher than any value the relationship provides. It may take days or months depending on the context, but look to eliminate these relationships altogether.

Negative contractors will surface no matter how your life is arranged. Optimizing happiness requires developing tools to manage both individual actions and entire relationships. This section has only just scratched the surface of tools for dealing with toxic relationships. If bad contractors have a strong influence in your life, I highly recommend seeking out additional resources on how to break or eliminate these patterns.

LEVERAGING GOOD CONTRACTORS

Luckily, while bad contracting is common, there are still good contractors out there. Leveraging these individuals makes building fortitude far easier. Good contractors assist in building your home while preventing you from damaging it as well. You always decide which blueprints are enacted, but creating a stable foundation is far easier when those around you are supportive. Leaning into and feeding these relationships pays huge dividends.

Good contractors are far less common than neutral or negative contractors simply because most people don't know how to empower and encourage those around them. The toolset simply doesn't exist. Instead, they offer assistance to the best of their abilities, which often becomes misguided and detrimental. Good contracting is a rare and valuable skill set. People even pay for it through occupations like coaching or therapy.

Good contractors, at their core, want the best for those around them and provide verbal support. That doesn't mean they always agree or bend to your will. In fact, the best contractors challenge assumptions, pushing for optimal paths and solutions. Even during the harshest challenges, they always validate worth and encourage achievement. Walking this line effectively is the primary criterion in distinguishing contractor quality.

Here's an example to help illustrate. Imagine working on a new song. A good contractor will ask questions about the intended audience, goals for the piece, and specific aspects you want feedback on. After understanding your goals and listening to the piece, they might say, "It's a good start. Much better than the first draft. The lyrics are still choppy, but I think another draft will smooth them out." They will never say, "Honestly, your music always sucks.

You should quit; you're just going to keep failing. Do accounting, you've always been good at that."

This example may seem clear-cut, but variants of the second comment are all too common. While well-intentioned, it completely undermines fortitude and is bad contracting. Good contractors learn what's important to you and work to enhance that, not what they think is best. If you're proud of an accomplishment, they delight in it with you, not minimize its impact. They push frames toward realism, productivity, esteem, and confidence. Constant exposure to these ideas significantly weakens internal barriers to optimizing happiness.

LOCATING GOOD CONTRACTORS

Knowing good contractors sounds nice, but where can you actually find them? Many people have encountered only a handful of good contractors, if any at all. Luckily, good contractors tend to congregate in certain places or around particular skills. By involving yourself in these same activities, you increase the chances of developing relationships with good contractors.

The most reliable way to encounter good contractors is by hiring them. It's typically easy to find coaches, therapists, and other similar occupations if you're willing and able to pay. The vast majority of these individuals are good contractors, as it's part of their job. Hiring a specialist can provide valuable examples of what to look for in other relationships. On the other hand, specialists are prone to errors just like everyone else, and the cost can be prohibitive.

A more wallet-friendly option is joining groups dedicated to personal development. Personal development is a broad phrase that can include a wide range of topics, like exercise, emotional regulation, and confidence, just to name a few. For our purposes, any group dedicated to improving some aspect of happiness (states or evaluations) qualifies. Individuals in these groups tend to intentionally cultivate support and betterment. Again, groups vary in quality, but finding good contractors is more likely in these circles than at random.

The simplest way to find more good contractors is simply to meet more people. This is so broad that it can essentially be done anywhere you encounter others. The hard part, for some, is proactively starting conversations and engaging. While it may not be a good fit for everyone, simply starting more conversations increases your chances of finding someone great. You can then invest more heavily in relationships that hint at good contracting. Meeting more people through virtual means is an option as well, as good contracting doesn't particularly require physical presence.

Finally, becoming a good contractor yourself tends to attract other good contractors. Supportive people prefer other supportive people. Few people find this natural, but the skill can be developed with effort and attention. We'll discuss how to be a good contractor soon, but expect to support others just as well as—or better than—they support you. Relationships are mutual.

Good contractors are more concentrated in a few places, but they can be anywhere. Pay attention to those who inspire and support you. Look for ways to deepen and enhance those relationships. Social circles influence not only your esteem and confidence but also your overall quality of life.

OTHERS BUILD HOMES AS WELL

Understanding homebuilding allows you to see how others construct confidence and esteem in their own lives. Knowing why someone feels fortitude or not is interesting, but the most practical application of this knowledge is to become a better contractor in others' homes. Each of your words and actions influences how others perceive themselves and, ultimately, how they perceive you. Few have considered this responsibility in-depth, so we'll focus on the exploration of others' fortitude here.

Imagine completely remodeling your home. Right now, it's uninhabitable and the entire foundation is rotten. You're committed to completing the project as quickly as possible, averaging twelve-hour days. The work is back-breakingly difficult. Progress is slow. The situation is dire. You reach out to your social network for help. Most do so happily. One person, however, always shows up with bags of garbage and leaves them on site.

It's strange behavior, and certainly not helpful, but you don't mind too much for the first few days. It hardly distracts from the project. After a few weeks of this behavior, however, it quickly becomes a burden. Removing trash takes time. It eats up valuable resources. Even if they occasionally take a bag or two home to help, their impact is skewed toward disruptive. How long before your frustration builds to the point that you demand they stop coming to "help"? How will that impact the relationship?

Whenever we judge, belittle, or dismiss others, we're bringing trash to their home. These behaviors threaten to destroy their fortitude, along with the relationship and your reputation. You wouldn't want trash dumped at your home, so you should extend the same courtesy to others.

WHY SHOULD I CARE?

Before exploring tactics for being a good contractor, let's investigate the value in generally doing what's best for others. Many individuals believe we should only invest in relationships where others will return the favor. In this section, we'll cover why you should always do what's best for others and help where you can, even from a purely selfish perspective.

You first need to disentangle the personal costs typically associated with helping others. Doing what's best for others can be independent of sacrificing your own needs and desires. I'm advocating helping others where you can, not putting yourself last. Factoring the personal costs into your decisions is reasonable. High-cost opportunities to help are discretionary based on relative value, but you should always act on low-cost opportunities.

For example, let's say you notice someone puzzling over a map at the train station. Offering to help them takes almost no effort if you know the routes. It only takes a few minutes, at most, to explain the best option. You would have spent this time waiting anyway. The cost of helping here is essentially zero, so you might as well do it.

Let's change the example. Again, you notice someone puzzling over a map at the train station. At the same time, however, your train pulls in. Helping will cause you to miss the train, which will make you an hour late to pick up your children from school. The cost of helping in this instance is much higher. You could still help, but it's likely not worth the trade-off.

This may seem like a straightforward comparison, but many individuals feel obligated to help others at great personal cost. I'd like to challenge that frame. You're not obligated to help when the costs far outweigh the benefits, nor should you feel guilty. Acting on these opportunities not only causes you unnecessary difficulty but can also fuel feelings of burnout and exploitation. Treating others well doesn't necessitate sacrificing yourself, just capitalizing on simple, low-cost opportunities.

Let's reconsider the original train scenario from the other side. You're lost in an unfamiliar city, trying to understand the complex transit system. Missing this train means missing an important interview. Without provocation, someone approaches to ask if you need help. What a huge relief! You accept, and they explain the best route. Your day became significantly better, and it cost them almost nothing.

These may seem like low-stakes examples, but these interactions matter. Arriving at an interview on time can be the reason someone gets a job. Treating others well can significantly improve moments, days, and even lives. In the context of homebuilding specifically, most opportunities are low-cost and offer substantial returns. You can support those around you at almost no cost to yourself.

Of course, others want help and support, but what's in it for me? Think of someone you don't know well but has helped you immensely. Would you be willing to do them a favor? If they asked for a specific type of specialist and you knew one, would you make the connection? How would you speak about them if someone asked about their reputation? If a person helped you, even if you hardly knew them, you're more inclined to reciprocate. We like those who treat us well.

Even if you don't want to be altruistic, habitually capitalizing on opportunities to help others builds your reputation and social capital. Those you help are more inclined to return the favor, with or without being asked. Helping others ultimately enriches your position.

Helping doesn't always pay back at a 1:1 ratio, we all know that from experience. *I just helped my friend move. Now he won't help me move! I should have never helped.* Not every act of kindness is reciprocated, and you shouldn't expect them to be. A mindset like "I helped this person cross the street, so they should buy one of my ebooks" hinges on external expectations and misses the point. Kindnesses are exchanged much differently than other kinds of transactions. The strategy here is value through volume, not individual, transactional acts.

Capitalizing on every low-cost opportunity spreads goodwill across a variety of individuals. Instead of hoping one or two of them have the exact skills or resources you need and return the favor, a shotgun approach is taken. With each instance, you increase the chance that someone will, at some point, reciprocate in a beneficial way. You may give directions hundreds of times and get nothing in return. But if even one stray individual connects you to a job opportunity or a new experience, you are net positive. The reputational benefits far outweigh the small increase in effort.

BECOMING A GOOD CONTRACTOR

With that in mind, let's return to good contracting. After the initial investment of developing baseline skills, building others' homes is extremely low-cost. You simply need to learn communication tactics that reliably produce an environment where others can build their fortitude. For esteem, that means feelings of importance, value, and worth. For confidence, it's feeling empowered and capable, along with a sense of progress. As with all contracting, individuals ultimately decide which blueprints are enacted in their home, but you can make it easier.

I'll assume you're genuinely interested in homebuilding, as that's the first and most necessary step. Intentions alone aren't enough. Others only know what they see and hear, not what's in your head and heart. You must choose the right tools to communicate your intentions effectively. While I'd love to explore communication in depth here, the topic is simply far too large. Instead, we'll focus on a few generally effective tactics for building fortitude in others.

Explicit Validation

Our first tactic is to explicitly acknowledge and validate what others say. For example, "Oh, you want to switch careers. I think that's a great idea." This may seem trivial and commonsensical, but many of us marginalize others and their ideas without realizing it, by either dismissing them or moving on. There's a huge difference between "That project sounds hard—way beyond your skill level. I'd never do it. I just don't see the point" and "That sounds like something my sister worked on. I could ask if she has any advice."

Explicit validation has two cornerstones. First, approach conversations with an intent of openness and curiosity. Focus on listening, looking for ways to validate the other person's experience. This doesn't mean you must agree, but just acknowledge you've heard what they said. Second, validate both the content and emotional quality of the experience: "It sounds like moving has been really challenging for you." This sounds simple, but it's often overlooked and makes a huge difference in creating an environment where others feel heard and valued.

Ask Questions

Asking questions for clarity and understanding also helps others feel heard and respected. Many of us habitually focus on our next opportunity to speak in conversations. The thought is that you don't want to forget an important thought, say something stupid, or lose the opportunity to be heard. While you're focusing on your next comment, however, you're not listening. This creates a low-quality conversation. When both individuals do this, it results in a disconnected ping-pong of semi-related sentences that can leave one or both feeling unheard and undervalued.

This tendency can be combated by asking questions for clarity and deeper understanding. "How did you pick that program? What's your plan for getting promoted?" Asking relevant questions proves you're listening and that you value what's being said. This requires balance, as you don't want every conversation to be an interrogation.

....

Training yourself to ask follow-up questions
forces you to pay attention and subtly
provides acknowledgment and validation.

....

Celebrate Effort

Celebrating effort and progress is another path to encouraging increased fortitude. When others pay attention to instances where effort worked to create positive outcomes, their belief in the connection grows. With this belief comes a tendency to keep trying. Effort is particularly emphasized here because it's always under your control, whereas individual outcomes may not be.

Praising others for effort, no matter how sizeable the accomplishment, encourages them to try more in the future. "Sure, you're not a millionaire, but you built twenty bikes from scratch and sold five. Six months ago, you only had the idea. I know it's not where you hoped to be, but that's serious progress!" I'm not advocating you ignore results entirely, but place them secondary to effort. Fortitude is about resilience and attempts, not perfect outcomes.

Even in cases where you think a project should be abandoned, you should still celebrate it. "You gave med school a full effort, but it doesn't seem like a good fit. I think you could invest that same drive in another field where you'll get better results." Realistic feedback is valuable and should be shared, but that doesn't mean it needs to be harsh. You can get the point across while also reinforcing someone's inherent value and encouraging effort.

Encourage Self-sufficiency

It's possible to become a good contractor in a way that certain people become dependent on you for all their fortitude needs. While flattering, this responsibility can be exhausting. In addition, their fortitude hinges on an external factor, your availability, which is risky. You can solve both these problems by sharing homebuilding tactics with them.

If someone relies on you for homebuilding, they trust your judgment. Use this relationship to suggest ideas and exercises which encourage self-sufficiency in increasing fortitude. We've covered several tactics, like sharing expertise or accomplishment journals, but there are countless others. It's an echo of the old proverb of "giving a fish" compared to "teaching to fish." You can create a good environment for increasing fortitude, but providing tools they themselves can use is far more effective.

We've only scratched the surface of communication, but the primer on these tactics should provide a starting point for becoming a good contractor. Unfortunately, exploring the nuances of communication is beyond the scope of this book. Communicating effectively, however, is a valuable skill that can streamline social interaction. Since the inability to achieve this is often a barrier to optimizing happiness, I highly recommend exploring additional resources at some point.

UNINTENTIONAL NEGATIVITY: THE CASE AGAINST SARCASM

Few of us intentionally dump trash into our loved one's landscapes. We typically have good intentions. Most of us have also stumbled into bad communication habits. The intent may be neutral or even positive, but that doesn't matter when your words, style, or tone implies otherwise.

Take a moment to reflect on your general communication style. Do you create an environment conducive to homebuilding? What do others say about your conversation style? Most importantly, is your communication effective? Does it create the outcomes you desire?

Most of us simply follow habits without considering their full impact. Without studying communication, seeing alternatives is difficult. In addition, these patterns seem to work well enough in most situations. Unfortunately, they also tend to dump trash in other people's landscapes. This comes in many flavors, but we'll focus on sarcasm because it's so common.

Imagine asking where the milk is at a grocery store. The cashier responds sarcastically, "Should I milk the cow and bake you cookies too? It's on aisle three." The text probably sounds snide, but the vocal context wouldn't make it agreeable either. Even a sweet or silly presentation wouldn't clarify between joking or mocking. On a good day, you might take it lightheartedly; on a bad day, as an insult.

Sarcasm may seem benign, but it can be problematic because it creates ambiguity and clouds intent: "Who cares? I'm only joking, lighten up!" Are you? What is your intent? Sarcasm is often used for jokes, but it's frequently used to indirectly mask insults as well. This makes it difficult, if not impossible, for listeners to accurately interpret intent. Each comment is open to interpretation. A negative interpretation means dumping trash. Effective, reliable communication tactics clarify intent instead of obscuring it.

"I like being sarcastic. I shouldn't have to change. Others should toughen up and stop taking everything so seriously." This position is both selfish and difficult to defend. What do you gain by using sarcasm as a tactic? Habitual ease? A sense of superiority? You risk degrading your relationships, reputation, and influence. Is that trade worthwhile? Better communication isn't about changing who you are. It's about using effective, reliable tactics.

"So, I should act like a character out of a show for toddlers? I can never be sarcastic?" Not exactly. The risk in sarcasm is communicating disdain or disapproval when it's not your intention. For one-off interactions, this can easily go wrong. Relationships with significant reserves of fortitude, however, have some flexibility. The receiver simply needs to know your overall underlying intent toward them is positive. Sarcasm can be used in proportion to the strength of the relationship.

Even then, however, you should be mindful. Constant sarcasm can leave even loved ones wondering what you truly believe. Consider it from your perspective. Let's say one friend continually insults your worth with comments like "Look at that, another screwup. What a surprise!" They always say it's a joke, but they never give genuine words of encouragement. How long until your confidence in their true feelings wanes? Investment in fortitude must far outweigh sarcastic jabs if you want to be safe, even if the intent is purely humorous.

I've used sarcasm as a scapegoat, but many communication tactics are used without contemplating the full impact. It's easy to make careless comments out of habit or ignorance. While unintentional, these comments impact those around you and your relationships as a whole. Paying even a little attention to tone, word choice, and style of speaking can pay huge dividends.

FIRST, BUILD YOURSELF A HOME

In this section, we've discussed the importance of home-building for yourself and others. A stable home, mapped to confidence and esteem, serves as the foundation for executing the rest of your blueprint. With a strong baseline belief in your worth and abilities, you're free to focus on taking action toward other goals.

Even if you've developed significant fortitude, however, occasional audits are worthwhile. Many find mastering confidence, esteem, and communication takes time, effort, and practice. While these processes make up a major part of this book, there's so much more to learn about these subjects. For many, homebuilding is the most important area for optimizing happiness. Additional research in this realm will only be beneficial.

With a stable home in place, you can focus on implementing other blueprint components. In the next section, we'll cover strategies for executing any project, regardless of the details. You've done enough planning. Now it's time to actually construct your mindscape according to your designs.

REFLECTION

The following set of questions is designed to help distill the ideas in this chapter. Take your time answering them and revisit any practices or exercises if you need to.

→ How would you describe yourself? Do the concepts trend positively or negatively?

→ What valuable attributes do you have?

→ What are your self-judgments like? Are your evaluations fair and neutral?

→ What accomplishments are you most proud of?

→ How often do you tackle new opportunities, even if they're challenging?

➜ How often do you challenge negative thoughts? How often do you empower them?

➜ What valuable skills and experiences do you have?

➜ What empowering affirmation fits you?

➜ Does your environment add or detract from fortitude?

➜ How often do others' actions make you feel bad? What can you do to be more independent?

➜ Do the people around you add or detract from your fortitude?

➜ How confident do you feel about your abilities?

➜ What are you currently putting effort into? What results do you expect?

➜ How often does fear of failure impact your execution of an idea?

➜ Where do you excel?

➜ What shareable expertise do you have?

➜ What quality of contractors are in your life?

6

LANDSCAPING –
EXECUTING GOALS

A plan without action is just wishful thinking. Think of someone you know who always has a plan but never takes action. How close are they to their goals? We can get some amount of enjoyment by simply talking about how to make things better, but it's short-lived. Action is what creates change. Accordingly, we'll spend this chapter focusing on how to consistently and efficiently take action toward your goals.

This chapter may seem more complex, but its goal is simple: execute behavior change. In reality, this tends to be difficult. The status quo is always easier to maintain than change. Doing nothing is the lowest-effort choice. However, if you want to optimize, you must break this default and devote time, energy, and effort to enacting your blueprint.

VALUE-ACTION TREES

Earlier, we briefly spoke about prioritizing values over habits and goals when creating a blueprint. Values are valuable as guides but useless without associated actions. You must tie the two together if you hope to influence happiness.

One of the easiest, clearest ways to do this is by imagining a tree with a value at the top. You can then draw branches from this value, subdividing it into goals and habits. Those can be further divided into smaller habits and goals until you reach specific actions. In the end, you can see exactly what it takes to enact your values.

We'll start at the top level with the value "I'm the type of person who helps others." From this value, you can branch into the goal of becoming a doctor. They're clearly connected, but becoming a doctor is a goal, not a specific action. There are many intermediate steps. You need to divide this goal into smaller goals or habits.

One step in becoming a doctor is to attend medical school, so you can create another branch with that goal. Getting into medical school is still a goal, not an action. You need another subdivision. What goals or habits get you into med school? The habit of studying regularly seems reasonable as it will be useful for entrance tests and during the program itself.

Studying regularly still isn't a specific action, though. You need to divide further. What goal or habit supports studying regularly? One option might be a goal of studying twenty minutes every day for a month. At this point, the goal is fairly clear and has an associated action. You've com-pleted one value-action chain.

One chain, however, might not be enough. At this point, you can add more branches to upstream habits and goals. For example, you could ask one doctor a month for advice on getting into medical school. The final product might look something like this.

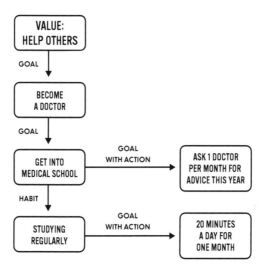

This is how one value can branch into a huge number of viable pathways. Now it's easy to visualize exactly how each action contributes to your values. Creating a value-action tree may seem daunting, but it's just breaking ideas into smaller, more manageable pieces. We'll cover more tactics for doing this later, but it tends to be easier than most peo-ple expect.

Value-action trees also make it easy to consider whether certain actions are contributing to desired life outcomes:

Is studying twenty minutes a day making studying more habitual? Then you simply follow the chain: Is studying improving my chances of med school entrance? Eventually, you reach the value: Does becoming a doctor fulfill my value of wanting to help people? If any of the answers are unsatisfactory, you can focus on other branches instead.

WORKING BACKWARD: ORPHANED GOALS AND HABITS

Value-action trees further highlight the merit of starting from values. Consider the goal of becoming a published author. Few branches can be spawned from this root. You can choose fiction or nonfiction, writing plans, novel-length, and topic, but options are limited when you consider goals first. The only way to achieve this path is to publish a book, which leaves many factors beyond your control.

Luckily, value-action trees make it much easier to work backward from orphaned goals to discover values. With visuals in hand, you can tunnel from an orphaned goal toward broader goals, habits, or values: Why do you want to become an author? What goal, habit, or value does it fill? Abstracting one level higher to something like "I enjoy sharing important ideas" opens significantly more branches. Audio and video are alternative routes if writing doesn't work out, for whatever reason.

Knowing possible moves across your value-action tree provides clarity in your options. It also avoids over-emphasis on any particular goal, especially those with external dependencies. Finally, it provides a visual representation of options, which many find easy to navigate when choosing ideal actions.

Don't be discouraged if the concepts in this section aren't completely clear yet. At this point, you're just aiming for comprehension of how goals, habits, and values interweave. The rest of the chapter covers how to create, maintain, and measure goals, actions, and habits in depth. Before moving on, however, try building a value-action tree. The more work you complete upfront, the easier subsequent exercises become.

HOW DO YOU CREATE HABITS?

Imagine two paths into town. One is well worn and familiar; you've traveled it thousands of times. Leaning on that experience, you continue taking it each day. You've never actually taken the second path, but supposedly it's roughly the same difficulty and leads to town as well. There are signs saying as much. Today you're late for work, which path are you more likely to take?

The well-traveled path is clearly the default choice. You're familiar with it, know what results to expect, and have successfully used it before. The other path is uncertain and offers no known benefit. So, let's tweak the scenario. What if you've heard the other route is faster? So much faster, you can avoid being late.

This information may pique your interest, but it's probably not enough to change your choice. The new path still has too much friction. *What if they're wrong and it's actually slower? What if the path is much more challenging? Maybe another time.* While the potential benefits might be known, you'll still refuse until you can increase certainty.

Even if you're brave enough to take the new path, you may become disheartened if there's a learning curve. For example, perhaps it takes five journeys to navigate the terrain. Most would be tempted to revert to the familiar route after only one or two attempts. The new path only becomes the default if you stay resilient while making it lower resistance, more enjoyable, and more familiar than the alternative.

We can think about habits similarly. The default is far easier than a new, desired action. You must make the desirable action easier, more enjoyable, and more frequent to increase your odds of choosing that action. With each success, that action becomes more routine and less difficult. You deepen the grooves of that path. Eventually, the desired action becomes the passive default instead of an active effort.

One of the primary drivers of habits is repetition. That means having goals for doing specific actions will create healthy habits. For example, studying twenty minutes a day for a month will reinforce a habit of studying regularly. We'll parse the nuances as we continue, but essentially, executing actions tied to smaller goals is how we complete larger goals, develop habits, and express values. This allows you to group all projects together and focus exculsively on executing goals with action steps, instead of differentiating by category.

PRIORITIZING GOALS

We've established that goals tied to specific actions are the underlying building blocks for blueprint execution, but how can you choose between projects? Any given blueprint likely has far more branches than can be tackled at once. You need a way to rank your endeavors and prioritize your efforts. Here are four different organization hierarchies. Which one you use depends on what feels most suitable at this point in your journey.

OVERALL IMPACT

Perhaps the best way of prioritizing goals is to judge the expected impact relative to their cost. This approach focuses on projects you believe in most, regardless of difficulty. Learning to tie your shoes faster might provide marginally more free time, but transitioning into a more fulfilling career has a far greater impact. It might be harder, but the optimal choice in this hierarchy is clear.

Prioritizing by impact typically starts with low-cost, quick wins: *I'm not sleeping well. Buying a new pillow should help a lot. I miss my weekly movie night. I'm blocking out time on the calendar right now.* If there are low-cost, high-reward opportunities in your blueprint, those should be tackled first. These projects are generally simple, can be completed swiftly, and have a positive impact.

Soon, however, you're faced with more challenging, higher-investment projects. The most common happiness barriers are deeply rooted in powerful frames, habits, relationships, and circumstances. While blueprints are specifically designed to work through these challenges, the process still requires significant effort. It can take months, years, or even decades to unwind and rebuild your life with optimal happiness in mind.

Prioritizing by impact forces you to face topics you have hitherto avoided or ignored. These are typically the most painful, complex, and challenging areas of life. Improving them generally requires facing unpleasant events and pushing far beyond your comfort zone. Many become frozen by the prospect of such an uncomfortable journey, undervaluing how much better the future will be afterward.

My history with meeting new people is a fitting example. I spent most of my life with few tools for creating pleasant social interactions with strangers. I especially lacked tools for building new, meaningful relationships. Each unsuccessful interaction built habits, frames, and tools which further cemented destructive frames. Before long, I intentionally avoided socializing with new individuals as much as possible.

My withdrawal meant limited experience with discomfort and fewer chances to try new tools. My skills deteriorated further. I justified the behavior as part of my character. I supplemented the belief with unreliable, defensive frames and values, like *I don't like other people* and *people are too stupid to understand me*. Somewhere beneath it all, however, I still wished I was better at connecting and that it came to me more naturally.

By chance, I eventually got exposure to more effective tools, like asking questions in conversations. Trying these tools drastically improved my results. Conversations flowed more freely and felt more connected. The weak frames I was using to avoid socializing cracked a little. It encouraged me to consume more resources. I kept learning, thus developing an effective toolset for most situations.

This process took years and many awkward conversations. If I'm honest, I'm still working on it. While there's room to improve my skills, I've progressed enough that this no longer hinders my happiness. I'm less anxious than before, and I know how to manage that anxiety far better. I know which situations will be easier or harder and how to prepare appropriately. These days I'm confident that I can navigate social interactions effectively. The change was challenging, but definitely one of the most important projects I've undertaken.

If you choose to prioritize by impact, start by considering which blueprint components will have the largest impact on your happiness. The most common high-impact changes, like diet, exercise, relationships, mental health, etc. have also been studied and explored extensively. If applicable, leveraging these existing resources can help convert high-level values into tangible goals and action steps.

One last note: prioritizing by impact requires clear desired outcomes and high resilience. Not everyone is in this position. I certainly wasn't when my mindscaping journey began. While thinking about impact is helpful, taking on problems that are too difficult too early can cause more harm than good. Progress is more important than perfection.

....

It's perfectly reasonable to build baseline
skills first, then tackle heavier projects.
It all depends on your circumstances.

....

APPROACHABILITY

Considering impact may be the most efficient measure, but it's not always the most realistic. It often makes more sense to gradually undertake projects of increasing complexity and difficulty. This creates the opportunity to build fundamental skills like planning and tracking before diving headfirst into demanding life changes. It also reduces the chance of burnout, quitting, and regression. It's completely reasonable to plant, grow, and care for a few flowers before committing to an entire farm.

Prioritizing by approachability means looking for challenging but realistic projects which build supplemental skills. For example, let's say health is in your blueprint. A very approachable project is something like flossing every night for a month. It doesn't come with years of emotional baggage or intense soul searching. It won't consume your thoughts each day. It just takes planning, tracking, and dedication.

Flossing may seem trivial, but reshaping any thought or behavior pattern, regardless of size, builds valuable skills for future endeavors. While details change, experimenting with your process for behavior change provides valuable insights across projects. You discover which methods produce action most consistently. You determine which tools resonate most strongly. As your skills and tools grow, so does the scope of the projects you're able to undertake.

On that note, you must keep increasing the scope of your projects for approachability to work. This method is about developing skills at a manageable pace, not focusing exclusively on easy projects. If you don't increase the scope, your skills will plateau, and so will your ability to optimize happiness. The most life-changing projects almost always require diverse, robust skills that can't be developed without stretching your comfort zone.

IMMEDIATE FUTURE IMPACT

The previous strategies assume a clear-cut blueprint, but it's possible your future vision is murky or missing intermediate steps. This is typical, especially in the beginning, and nothing to be worried about. It's important, however, that you start taking action as soon as possible to develop familiarity with the process. If this sounds familiar, consider prioritizing immediately useful projects.

Taking on board all the information in this book, designing a lifelong vision, and making optimal choices is demanding. In the early stages, the breadth and depth of planning, organizing, and deciding can feel overwhelming, but you don't need a perfect blueprint to start optimizing happiness. You can simplify immensely by picking one project for the immediate future. This allows progress to be made while providing additional time to work through the planning stages.

Perhaps the easiest way to plan for the immediate future is to consider one project that will be useful in the next thirty days. There's no need to overthink it; simple goals are great. A few examples are drinking more water, focusing on better posture, or doing a kind act daily. There's no wrong answer here. The goal is simply taking action and experiencing the change process.

If the month ends and your blueprint is still muddy, consider another cycle of prioritizing by immediate usefulness. It's perfectly rational to work through immediate projects while refining a rich blueprint. As you gain experience, don't be afraid to experiment with factors like timeline and project difficulty. When your blueprint is clearer, you can increasingly introduce goals tied to values.

RANDOMNESS

In many cases, optimizing choices can be hard, if not impossible. When all the choices seem good, which one is best? There's often no way to know. You simply have to make a choice. If all projects seem equally good, you can leave the decision to chance. This may sound risky, but it's preferable to inaction and overanalysis, which halts progress. The choice may not be perfectly optimized, but it at least creates momentum and experience.

There is an infinite number of ways to live: *Should I start a business? Quit my job? Take up yoga? Move to the city?* This huge number of options makes determining the absolute best life impossible. Some people endlessly gather information to combat this uncertainty, expecting certainty before moving forward: *Should I buy a new car? Maybe I'll do just a little more research on the best brand.*

In some instances, this research can be useful. At a certain point, however, research hits diminishing returns. There's no definitive answer to whether moving to another country or going back to school will produce a better life. Much of the time, you can't know until you've made a decision and lived through the experience.

You should be strategic about major life choices and do your due diligence, but sometimes it's impossible to determine a clear preference. If it's that hard, you expect the outcomes to be roughly equally good. It's essentially like picking between $10,000.01 and $10,000.02. Further research won't change the value of each option; it only consumes precious time. Any choice is better than inaction.

Making a choice using randomization is simple. Enumerate and number the projects you're considering. Ensure each of them is something you're willing to commit to. Then find a random way to pick one—the easiest of which is a random number generator. The goal that emerges is the one you focus on. No second-guessing, backing out, or re-drawing. Those tactics are often used to stall and fruitlessly analyze more.

This may seem ridiculously simple, but when you can see so many ways to live, indecision is a very common happiness blocker. If all choices are positive, continual analysis is the worst option as it's the status quo. Choosing a project randomly is a surefire way to overcome this analysis paralysis. After starting, you can always switch projects if you feel like it isn't producing positive results.

TYPES OF LANDSCAPING TOOLS: ACTION AND SYSTEM

Once you've decided on a project, successful execution depends on the tools you choose. Generally, there are two types of implementation tools: system and action. System tools enhance consistency in taking action. Action tools are the specific steps chosen to achieve goals. We'll explore action tools first, as they tie directly into the value-action hierarchy.

ACTION TOOLS

Action tools are the actions you choose with the intent of fulfilling a value or goal. Let's say your goal is to become a world-class sprinter. Action tools that potentially contribute to that goal are things like lifting weights, sprinting, running marathons, reading about sprinting, or looking for a mentor. Unfortunately, this book can't possibly cover the best action tools for every possible goal. There are simply too many options and combinations.

We can, however, focus on heuristics for choosing action tools. These heuristics guide you toward tools that are likely to be both efficient and effective. Since actions largely determine outcomes, choosing the right action tools is vital for progress and success.

PRIORITIZING: GENERALIZABILITY AND RESEARCH

The number of action tools available for any single goal can be overwhelming: *I want to own a business. Do I study marketing, develop a product, start a service, or look for a co-founder?* Hundreds of branches can be created from that goal, but they can't all be pursued. Fortunately, you can use general efficacy, research, and reputation as proxies for experience and prioritize that way.

One way to distinguish tools is generalizability, meaning many individuals have experienced success using them. Meditation, for example, has a stronger reputation for decreasing stress than painting your forehead purple, even if you can find advocates for both. If a tool has worked for tens of thousands or millions of people, it's likely to help you as well.

Popularity can be a good sign, but don't blindly accept popular tools at face value. This is especially true of tools that have quickly and recently become popular. New, trendy tools tend to be under-researched and over-marketed. How many fad diets were later determined to be unhealthy? When possible, use action tools that have stood the test of time. They're more likely to be effective.

Renown is a good indicator, but it should be cross-referenced with expertise. The logical or scientific foundation of tools provides more context on its expected efficacy. Some popular action tools are debunked after even surface-level research. For example, consider the idea of spot reducing fat by exercising muscles in the same area. This seems reasonable, but studies show that's not how fat loss works. You can find this opinion scattered about, but it's definitely not an ideal action tool. The best tools are often extensively researched and supported by experts.

Unfortunately, many action tools aren't well researched. They may be worth trying, but be cautious of the risks in unexplored realms. Weigh this risk against your goal's importance and expected impact. Physical safety is rarely a concern, but time, money, and energy are valuable expenditures. Most action tools are safe enough to try, but use common sense and opt for well-founded tools where possible.

Generalizability and research won't cover every tool, but they're good rules of thumb if you don't know where to start. If they don't work, don't hesitate to explore and experiment. Your unique mindscape may require obscure or atypical tools to accomplish your goals. This section is merely about prioritizing based on the probability of usefulness, not setting strict boundaries.

DETERMINING TOOL EFFECTIVENESS

The primary purpose of action tools is to achieve corresponding goals. Each tool has varying degrees of usefulness, based on interactions with your mindscape and effective progress toward accomplishing the task at hand. While estimation is possible, knowing how useful a tool is generally requires trying it. A knife might sound like a good tool for producing lumber until you actually try it. Pay attention to how much progress action tools create.

This may seem like common sense, yet many individuals habitually use ineffective tools for long periods. Consider the individual who has been exercising and dieting for months without results. They weigh the same, aren't stronger, and don't feel healthier. Clearly, their action tools aren't working. Your results don't need to be grand or sudden, but tools should be revisited if your effort doesn't produce progress.

This trap seems especially common for those using popular tools. While social proof generally indicates tools worth trying, it doesn't guarantee the tool is a good fit for your mindscape. *Waking up at 5 a.m. has always left me groggy for four hours, but it works for her! I must be doing it wrong. It'll work for me eventually!* That's not a realistic viewpoint. What works for others may not work for you.

Be especially cautious of individuals touting one tool as a panacea. It may solve multiple problems for them, but not for everyone. An ice pick may solve many problems in their tundra but won't do much in your rainforest. This is how a tactic like meditation can be completely life-changing for some and mostly fruitless for others. The efficacy of a particular action tool relies on your individual mental composition.

Before writing a tool off, however, ensure you've made a genuine attempt to use it correctly. This means diligently following through, not dismissing it half-heartedly when it becomes inconvenient. Blaming the tool after inconsistent effort is common and misguided. It allows you to avoid difficulty at the cost of stagnation. Action tracking, which we'll discuss later, provides insight into whether it's your efforts or the tool itself that is likely at fault.

As an example of this process, let's take the goal of landing a paid public-speaking gig. You come up with the sub-goal of increasing the clarity of your message. As a corresponding action tool, you decide to write a new twenty-minute speech each week for a month. Let's fast forward to the end of the month. If you haven't written four speeches at the end of the month, consistency is a problem. Assuming the writing is done, you can analyze your progress toward the goal. How much closer are you to landing a paid gig?

Say you haven't vocalized your speeches anywhere, not even to yourself. It seems unlikely this path will lead to your desired outcome. You need another supplementary action tool or another path. Let's say that next month, you also send the speeches to event planners. At the end of that month, you land two unpaid bookings. The goal hasn't been achieved, but progress is definitely happening. The combination of these two actions is far more likely to eventually produce the desired outcome. We'll discuss analyzing progress more throughout the chapter, but it's a good time to start considering the implications of efficacy on tool choice.

UPDATE YOUR ARSENAL CONSTANTLY

Even if your chosen tools create progress, it's worth experimenting occasionally. Imagine the project of digging holes. Your current tools are great, or so you think. You're using a spade to dig fifty-foot holes and a plastic bag to haul dirt. If you assume those are good enough, you'll never find out about shovels or wheelbarrows. Even functional tools can have better alternatives, but you'll never know without exploration and experimentation.

Most high-level goals are multi-faceted, so approach them from several angles, using various action tools. For example, say you're working on tempering your responses during strong emotions. You took an anger management class, which mainly taught walking away as early as possible. That might work for some circumstances, but what about situations you can't leave? What about when you're feeling an emotion other than anger? This tool likely isn't enough, and you should explore further.

Relying on only one or two tools typically creates a shallow understanding of the realm. For some goals, this is fine. For others, especially mastery or permanent habits, a wide set of tools is necessary to cover all relevant circumstances. By slowly locating, trying, and analyzing new tools, you can mix and match them across scenarios, occasionally replacing old tools with better ones. This provides far more flexibility and efficiency than any single tool.

Locating new tools is relatively easy. Start with high-level research for common solutions to your problem. Take wanting higher-quality sleep, for example. There are countless resources for improving sleep quality: articles, books, expert interviews, courses, etc. Consume a few of these information sources, extract actions that seem useful, and keep working toward your desired outcomes.

Here's a personal example to illustrate the process. Long before coming up with the idea of mindscaping, I heard that daily gratitude journals increased happiness. It sounded reasonable, so I got a journal and wrote in it consistently for two months. Nothing changed. I consulted with others who had used the tactic successfully. The response was that I hadn't done it long enough. I continued writing in it consistently, even though my progress and results were lacking.

After four months, I still felt the same as when I started. Identifying nice-sounding events came more quickly, but I didn't feel happier. I didn't even feel more grateful. Around the same time, I encountered visualizing good daily events as an alternative gratitude-building tool. Both tactics seemed roughly the same, but I figured it was worth trying.

After only one session, my results were completely different. Seeing the event in my mind produced the feeling of gratitude I was searching for. Within days I saw the value in creating a gratitude practice. A small shift in tools made all the difference. Changing tactics after poor results is an elementary idea. Even though I knew this logically, however, I didn't think to actively seek out alternative or supplemental tools.

You can save yourself a lot of time by proactively acquiring new action tools. Instead of struggling, waiting, and hoping, create a plan with multiple potential action tools, or at least know where you can find more. Tools don't need to be swapped often, but occasional tweaks can produce substantial results. In addition, you'll know alternatives for tools that turn out to be ineffective. Otherwise, you'll never know if you have a spade or a shovel.

MASSIVE LANDSCAPE-SHIFTING TOOLS: MAPPING TOOLS TO TIME

You can dig a hole with your hands, a shovel, or a drilling machine. Which one is best depends on how big you want the hole and how much you can invest. Some tools are designed to have more impact but come at a higher cost of time, money, or intensity. Action tools work in the same way. The scope of your project determines the necessary tool strength.

Much of this book has described mindscaping as a slow-marching, continuous process. That's true for the process as a whole, but individual projects are more nuanced. It is possible to create rapid change in a constrained realm, although it requires heightened investment. Combining factors like expertise, structured environments, immersive time commitment, and willingness to weather emotional difficulty opens the possibility of massive change. The question is whether the expected benefits outweigh the costs.

High-impact, high-cost tools sound nice, but their use is contingent on being able to pay for them. When you invest heavily in one area, you ultimately pay in others. The most powerful tools have the potential to disrupt balance or exceed your resources in time, money, or emotional resilience. On the other hand, some goals can only be achieved with powerful tools.

Rehab centers and bootcamps are examples of powerful, landscape-shifting tools. These programs essentially force unfettered focus on a single project. Distractions are extremely limited. Daily life is replaced with a new, controlled context. Experts provide continuous coaching, implementing a rigorous curriculum. A financial investment may be required, as well. These tools demand a heavy price with the promise of an equivalent reward.

Depending on your circumstances, a landscape-shifting tool might sound promising. Approach wisely, as great outcomes are possible but not guaranteed. Not everyone is well-positioned to benefit relative to the costs. Before investing heavily, spend some time on your self-survey, ensuring your situation is a good fit. Mapping tools to costs reduces the risk of investing resources beyond what you can actually afford.

These are extreme examples, but tools vary across the intensity spectrum. If you're not sure about investing in a high-cost tool like an isolated retreat, consider a mid-level investment like coaching or a low-cost investment like a book. These are far easier to adjust to and require fewer upfront resources. At the same time, they may not produce the depth or speed of results you're looking for.

There is no best tool strength; this section aims to make you aware of options for intensity, investment, and pacing. If you want better posture, a three-month retreat is probably overkill. If you're struggling with clinical depression, reading a positive quote every day probably isn't enough. The best choice depends on your resources and the urgency and importance of your project.

SYSTEM TOOLS

Action tools provide a clear target, but they don't increase follow-through. For that, you need system tools. System tools are ideas, strategies, and tactics for increasing consistency with action tools. These tools generally work across projects, making execution easier and more manageable. Don't expect to simultaneously implement every system tool covered in this section. Instead, layer them according to what's most needed for your mindscape.

CRAFTING YOUR DECISION ENVIRONMENT

Imagine standing on a pathway that forks in two. One trail is muddy and unkempt. It's also blocked by a fence. The other trail is smooth and paved. Which are you more likely to choose? The answer is clear, with implications for how you should structure your environments. If you can make the desirable path appealing and enact roadblocks everywhere else, making the preferred choice becomes easy.

We'll cover many ways of adjusting friction in enacting a particular action, but let's start with an example. Let's say you struggle with overeating sweets. If you see them, you habitually eat them. Always. Unfortunately, it's also making you unhealthy. Clearly, this behavior produces undesirable states. You need more resistance on the path of eating sweets.

Currently, you decide while seeing the stimulus: *This candy looks good; should I eat it? Definitely!* Deciding at this point is waiting until the undesirable path is at its clearest, the impulse is at its strongest. You may occasionally abstain through pure willpower, but how consistently? If this decision is made further upstream, at an easier point, the preferred path becomes far more desirable.

For example, maybe refraining from buying sweets comes easily. Accordingly, upstream behavior can be more easily modified by implementing a new rule: I don't buy sweets at the grocery store or keep them at the house. Later at home, the downstream decision to eat sweets has far more friction. First, the visual triggers are gone, reducing impulses. Second, if those impulses show up, they're far harder to satisfy. Leaving the house is far more effort than walking to the kitchen. You've essentially erected a fence on the pathway to sweets.

This helps, but it doesn't ensure perfect behavior. You might drive to the store if you're craving sweets enough. The default, however, has shifted toward the desirable path. There's significantly more friction in making the undesirable choice, which will reduce its frequency. Carefully crafting your environment to create nudges like this can drastically alter your choices and outcomes.

This idea can be applied to a wide range of situations: *I'll leave my credit card at home when shopping and just take cash, so I can only spend a set amount. I'll put a note on my bathroom mirror so when I see it in the morning, I'll remember to take my vitamins. I'll set my computer to power off automatically at 10 p.m., so I go to bed.* And so on. Doing this across a number of upstream decisions can radically alter your daily decision ecosystem.

Crafting your decision environment shifts effort away from discipline toward planning, which is far more reliable. To find environment-shaping opportunities tunnel through behaviors looking for potential upstream, low-willpower adjustments. Start with the situation, then consider what factors lead to that decision and how you might influence them. Typically, there are at least a few easy upstream choices you can make.

The rest of this chapter is about other ways of making desired choices that lead to the path of least resistance. Most tactics for influencing behavior are less direct than working in decision trees and require effort. Using these tactics may not feel like the path of least resistance. Instead, they pave the way for making other desired choices. You trade effort in an easier area for reduced effort in a harder one.

Think of it as the two pathways from the earlier example. Erecting a fence in front of the clear path takes an effort. Clearing mud from the other path also requires work. It takes some investment to make the desired path more appealing, but taking that path becomes much easier in the future. This parallel can be a useful reminder as we discuss other system tools. Resistance to using system tools may be rooted in the effort needed to clear the desired path, not in using the tools themselves.

STAYING MOTIVATED

We're most likely to make aspirational plans when already feeling highly motivated: *I'm inspired! This year I'm going to get healthy, rich, and happy.* Unfortunately, motivation often disappears when ambition meets reality. Excitement wanes as roadblocks, struggles, and detours emerge. Soon, execution happens purely through willpower, if at all. Maintaining consistent, disciplined action without any underlying motivation generally leads to exhaustion and failure.

There's no way to feel completely motivated all the time, that's just not how feelings work. It is possible, however, to feel motivated more often. The rest of this subsection discusses different ways to feel more desire toward your desired path. These tactics shift motivation into more controllable channels, which means pure willpower, a more difficult and expensive tool, will be necessary less often.

Make your Why Clear and Visible

Planning goals feels great, but it's easy to lose sight of the big picture during individual moments of implementation. Leaving bed to exercise is hard now, and being fit won't appear until later. Impulses to sacrifice desirable future states are strongest in the moment: *I'll just have one more drink. I'll relax and skip working on my book today.* These moments create goal debt, and just like financial debt, the amount due eventually builds to substantial problems.

Momentary impulses can be powerful, especially if you don't have good reasons for acting against them: *It's just one cookie, why not?* One way to combat these tendencies is by creating clear reasons and keeping them visible. This brings all of the full impacts of your choice to mind, not just the most salient ones. Simply remembering good reasons for a particular action can be enough of a nudge to change the decision.

Reasons should spawn naturally in the process of refining a value-action tree: "I want to eat healthy because I will feel better, live longer, and have more energy for loved ones." These reasons must also be personally meaningful and emotionally compelling to be effective. If not, they won't be useful in influencing your choice. Before settling on a motivating reason, make sure the long-term net positive is clear.

There are several pathways to uncovering meaningful reasons for choosing a specific goal. Start by tunneling into how the goal relates to your values and why that's important to you:

— *I want to get married.*

— *Why?*

— Because my parents think I should be married by now.

This is externally based, making it unreliable and harder to develop feelings for.

—I want to buy a house.

—Why?

—It contributes to my value of growth and will provide a greater sense of mastery, autonomy, and safety.

These are clear, compelling reasons which are internally motivated. It will be much easier to feel purposeful about this goal. If a goal fails to produce any internally inspiring reasons, it's worth reconsidering if it belongs in your blueprint.

Another option for producing stronger feelings is visualizing outcomes for each decision. Once you've settled on a goal that makes sense logically, spend a few minutes imagining the first-person experience for each pathway. For exercising consistently, you might imagine an average day a year from now, comparing both pathways. These images can later lend emotional weight to logical ideas and help combat in-the-moment pressures.

A clear and compelling reason is only useful if it's present in your thoughts. You can increase the likelihood of remembering these reasons during crucial choices by increasing visual reminders in commonly seen places. For increasing exercise, you might write: *"I exercise to live healthi-*

er, longer" on a whiteboard in your room. Alternatively, you could put a sticky note with a similar message on the door frame. Another option is changing the background of your phone or computer.

Finding good reasons and keeping them in mind provides ammunition for pushing back against undesirable impulses. While you probably won't remember or be swayed in every instance, these tactics are all about nudges in the right direction.

> The desired path is far more appealing when you know exactly why you want to take it.

Create Social Accountability

While external influences are detrimental in determining values, they can be highly valuable in taking action. Other people can contribute a fresh perspective to tunneling, encourage desirable action, hold you accountable, and share the experience of working toward similar goals. Social forces, aimed in the right direction, can drastically alter which path seems easiest.

There are many options for creating social accountability, such as classes, clubs, groups, coaching, and so on. There are even services specifically dedicated to charging you money when you fail to take action toward goals.

While these are all viable options, we'll focus on regular check-ins with someone trustworthy and supportive, as it's one of the most accessible tactics.

Regular check-ins are fairly easy to start. Select a trusted companion and set a regular time to meet, with the explicit intention of discussing goal progress. During each session, focus on what went well, what needs work, and goals for the next meeting. Most commonly, both individuals discuss their progress, but one-way sessions work as well. It's typical to meet once a week, but should be tweaked to your personal situation, as always.

Regular check-ins create a time-bound obligation to present tangible progress, another person to refine ideas with, and dedicated time to focus on improving. This is generally much faster than working alone because barriers are identified and removed more effectively. It's why trainers, therapists, and other similar professionals can be so helpful. Also, regular check-ins don't require any level of expertise to be effective. An empowering, reliable partner can provide sufficient support for most projects. You just need to locate the right person.

Anyone you check in with must at least have your best interests at heart, be supportive, and provide feedback without attacking your character. The ideal partner asks powerful questions about progress, calls you out when you're stalling, and challenges you to rise to your potential. A second opinion and gentle prodding encourages most people to create far more than they ever could alone.

The principles for choosing individual accountability partners apply equally to groups. The only difference is most individuals feel pressure proportionate to the size of the group. One person pushing you is a nudge, fifty feels more like a shove. This makes an accountability group's quality even more important. In the ideal case, you'll share a wealth of experience and resources. Many individuals mean many perspectives from which to solve problems.

In the worst case, social pressures are largely destructive, with individuals being targeted, ignored, or otherwise mistreated. Instead of enhancing, the culture pushes everyone to degrade each other's aspirations. This not only slows growth in that particular realm but also threatens the homebuilding process. Unfortunately, these environments are fairly common. Choose the groups you spend time with wisely. They're more influential than you might think.

We mostly focused on regular check-ins, but there are many other tactics for creating external accountability. Regardless of the specific flavor you choose, exploring goals with like-minded individuals typically makes execution much easier and more enjoyable. Investing time into surround yourself with individuals who help optimize your happiness is almost always worthwhile.

Create Rewards

It's a very widely held belief that rewards boost motivation. If that's the case, offering yourself rewards should work just as well, right? On the surface, self-rewarding for action seems logical, but it's not entirely straightforward. Saying, "If I eat healthy for a month, I can spend $300 on whatever I want" may or may not motivate you. It depends on the context.

First, let's talk about why rewards are useful in the first place. As previously discussed, sometimes, setting yourself up for future pleasure requires unpleasantness in the present. Exercising or taking a stressful job to provide for a family are clear examples. While these trades are generally deemed worthwhile, the moments you actually pay for them can be exhausting. When the balance feels especially skewed toward undesirable, you're more likely to quit and choose another path.

Self-reward introduces an arbitrary pleasant state to break unpleasant streaks and make the whole situation more manageable. This is where context becomes important. The original goal must be meaningful, and the reward must provide respite from the necessary difficulty. The prospects of a shopping spree won't convince you to start eating healthy if there's no underlying motivation. Rewards are a way of producing different desirable states, not making purposeless actions desirable.

Assuming your goal is tied to purpose, even simple rewards can increase motivation. For example: *For every five hundred words I write, I'll take an extra ten-minute break; If I work out consistently for two weeks, I'll treat myself to a smoothie.* Again, you're creating small, immediate, desirable states both as tangible objects to look forward to and as a break from other necessary work. If the foundation is solid, these small injections of happiness can make even the hardest goals more bearable.

Creating Rewarding Emotional States

Most of us default to some tangible object or physical experience when thinking of rewards—new clothes, a massage, a nap. While these types of rewards serve a purpose, they're dwarfed in comparison to experiencing a rewarding emotional state. Finding ways to make desired choices immediately produce gratification makes them borderline addictive and hugely influential.

Perhaps the easiest way to create rewarding emotional states is by being aware of your efforts and pausing every now and then to take pride in them. Many people skip between tasks without ever acknowledging any accomplishment. While it may feel unnatural at first, take a few moments after any particularly difficult choice to relish your progress. This helps tie progress to desirability and increases the odds you'll take the desired action again.

Some individuals also see results from creating arbitrary celebrations tied to desired actions. Typically, this takes the form of something like a dance, affirmation, or shared moment. Another option is tracking, which we'll discuss in depth later. Many individuals derive pleasure from seeing progress against historical data and breaking personal bests. For the more numerically-inclined, this is a great approach.

Figuring out how to derive emotional pleasure from useful action is one of the strongest tools at your disposal. Unguided, these mechanisms often create negative habits with immediate emotional gratification and negative long-term results. With direction, you can use this process to make taking desired actions with positive long-term results exponentially easier. If you only invest in a few tools, this should be a strong contender.

PUNISHMENTS AND CONSEQUENCES

We can't talk about rewards without considering punishments as well. Many individuals think they can guilt, beat, or scare themselves into making desired choices. While it may be the only tool they have, better ones certainly exist. Internally-based, arbitrary punishments are an unreliable source of motivation and likely to backfire, damaging your home. Here are a few reasons why punishments are generally an ineffective system tool.

REDUCED FOLLOW-THROUGH

Punishments are meant to incite actions through the threat of unpleasant experiences. If you're not executing purposeful, life-improving actions, though, why would you execute a self-imposed unpleasant punishment? Anyone avoiding action in one area seems likely to avoid action in the other. If you're somehow capable of enforcing only punishments, don't waste your time creating unnecessary, unpleasant experiences. Instead, tunnel into the methods and frames you're using for punishments and apply them to goals instead.

If you choose self-punishment, failing to follow through can also reduce confidence and esteem. Punishment essentially adds a failure condition to something inherently demoralizing. It also emphasizes results over process and introduces additional self-judgments: *I can't follow through with anything. I just can't. I always fail. I give up.* Essentially, it undermines many of the efforts you're making toward optimizing happiness.

ENLIST OTHERS TO ROOT AGAINST YOU

I'll have friends hold me accountable to the punishment, then I'm sure to follow through. This is even more precarious than self-imposed punishments. Social accountability can be helpful, but an adversarial frame is likely to compromise the project and/or the relationship. The punishment is more likely to materialize this way, but with far higher stakes than necessary.

External punishment enforcement can easily strain relationships, even if conditions are clearly outlined beforehand. Having a negative experience imposed on you, even if it was your idea, can create resentment. For them, it can create guilt or fear of following through. Worst of all, many punishments actively pit others against you: "If I eat chocolate this week, I'll give you $200." In these situations, you're incentivizing others to be poor contractors, potentially undermining your homebuilding efforts.

Accidentally creating an adversarial punishment also pushes your focus externally. At a certain point, the intensity of consequences starts outweighing internal motivation and the goal's original intent. Fabricating data or otherwise cheating becomes more appealing. This creates the risk of wasting time faking productivity to avoid punishment, completely reversing the original intent.

This may seem unlikely at first glance, but the same actions are common in similarly structured competitions, like weight loss, athletics, or work productivity quotas. Winning, proving worth to others, or simply avoiding negative consequences can push you toward unethical actions while undermining the intrinsic value of the desired action.

We've covered a number of reasons why punishments are generally unreliable foundations for motivation. In fairness, though, it doesn't always play out this way. Punishments can be useful, especially for those who are naturally competitive. The details, however, are critically important. For most people, most of the time, the potential pitfalls outweigh the benefits. Enlisting others for support is far more reliable and should be experimented with before external punishments are ever considered.

THE DOUBLE-POSITIVE PUNISHMENT

Occasionally, individuals implement a hybrid reward-punishment, sometimes called a double-positive punishment. The core idea is to create some positive outcome regardless of your individual results toward achieving a goal. *If I fail this test, I'll give $100 to charity.* The idea is to create motivation while also improving the world if self-discipline fails. Although this seems reasonable on the surface, the logic in using double-positive punishments as motivation is flawed.

To be clear, I don't think double-positive punishments are a net negative for the world. Donating to charity, cleaning your parent's house, or any other prosocial but unpleasant task provides value, and it's better than self-inflicted, needless suffering. The problem is this punishment provides competing incentives against your original goal. While still productive in a sense, this extra option allows you to work on low-impact projects instead of actually optimizing happiness.

The thought process that undermines motivation looks like this: *I don't feel like exercising today. Skipping means I have to donate to charity. Oh well. That's still good for the world, even if it costs money.* It's more meaningful than doing nothing, but donations aren't a substitute for health-improving actions. Double-positive punishments essentially create a desirable secondary path that dilutes the higher-impact primary path.

Even worse, this secondary path can easily become the path of least resistance, allowing you to indefinitely avoid working toward a particular goal. Sure, something gets done, but not the highest priority steps. Focusing exclusively on a primary goal tends to be more effective than splitting your attention with another, slightly unpleasant, and less important goal.

NOT OPTIMIZING HAPPINESS

Perhaps the most serious problem with punishments is that they directly contradict the goal of optimizing happiness. Arbitrary punishments introduce potentially unpleasant experiences into your life with few, if any, tangible benefits. Implementing change is hard. Mistakes are common. It makes far more sense to embrace the process than to further limit your happiness when you don't reach perfection.

The world naturally creates consequences for inaction, so you don't need punishments. You must live through the results of your choices. For example, *I always fight with my partner. If I don't learn how to communicate better, the relationship is at risk. I don't want to lose them.* Natural punishments are typically far more motivating than artificial ones. These are the consequences worth focusing on.

Extra punishments can produce immediate fear, but natural, long-term consequences can be made to feel just as painful. Consider using visualization, tunneling, or other similar tools to increase the salience of these impacts:

If I don't get healthy, I'll feel too tired to spend quality time with my loved ones. I'll use my savings on expensive doctor's bills, which means I'll be working far beyond retirement age. I won't get the chance to travel like I've always wanted. These consequences have tangible effects on quality of life and happiness.

To be clear, there are times where punishments can provide motivation. They work for some people in certain circumstances. Typically, these instances are externally imposed, carefully calculated for value, and calibrated to specific mindscapes. Most often, however, they're prone to backfire in a number of ways. Other options tend to be more effective and more reliable. Before choosing punishment as a form of motivation, consider all potential negative implications. If you're at all unsure, leave punishments as a secondary or tertiary tactic.

MISTAKES ARE NOT FAILURES

Imagine installing a new door in your home. Your first attempt isn't quite right, the angle is awkward. Would you say, "Forget it, this door isn't worth it"? What if it's the front door, allowing the elements and insects into your home? Chances are you'd try again. The benefits of a properly mounted front door far outweigh the cost of another attempt. This may seem like a simple example, but you may do the opposite in your mindscape, taking on important projects only to jump ship at the slightest misstep, possibly damaging your home in the process.

Many of us cling to unreasonable standards of perfection. We frame the tiniest mistake as a failure. Those examples are then used to project a lack of future success as well. Life doesn't actually work this way. Being unable to run a mile today says nothing about tomorrow. Each consecutive attempt builds experience and increases your chances of future success. Mistakes and missteps don't derail future prospects unless you let them.

Imagine driving along a highway. You accidentally miss the exit for your destination. How would you solve this problem? The simple answer is to take the next exit. It's slightly further from your destination, but it's the only way to actually get there. Why not apply this logic to mistakes when taking action toward your goals? Giving up after one failed action is like missing an exit, then intentionally skipping another thirty exits out of frustration. It makes no sense.

This framework's effectiveness hinges on considering mindscaping as a continuous, flexible project. Mistakes cannot cause failure, only quitting and self-judging labels can. You'll feel much better by approaching mindscaping with the understanding that it takes time, effort, and dedication. Many paths are nonlinear and deviate from your original plans. Life, and especially optimizing happiness, tends to be messier than we'd like.

It may be a cliché, but treating mistakes as learning opportunities is truly a useful frame. We can always learn from our failure to take action or from lackluster results. Tunnel into the root causes, looking for potential solutions: *How can I take action next time? Which changes in my thoughts, action, or environment will help most?* Looking for actionable steps helps shift your thinking away from dwelling on negative emotions and on to useful future ideas.

Framing mistakes as learning also eliminates self-judgment and potential damage to your home. Accepting mistakes as an expected and inevitable part of the process allows for a faster release of the associated negative emotions. Training yourself to habitually frame actions this way takes time, but it's far more useful than expecting perfection. Progress doesn't require a perfect record, just more hits than misses. Every step forward counts.

FOLLOW THROUGH

The next set of system tools focuses on making intended actions clear, easy, and efficient. Motivation tools make you feel like you should take action, while follow-through tools ensure you know exactly which action to take. Determining actions beforehand reduces in-the-moment temptations, increasing your likelihood of taking the desired action. Follow-through system tools may take time to set up, but they tend to pay back several times over.

MINIMUM REQUIRED ACTION

Motivation system tools increase the feeling's frequency, but they aren't a guarantee. Some days we simply won't feel like taking action. In many cases, there's much to be gained by pushing through these feelings and acting anyway. One option for guaranteeing progress is imposing a small minimum required action that must be taken regardless of feelings.

The key to creating an effective minimum required task is choosing a task so small that execution is almost effortless. If it sounds easy, you can confidently commit to taking that action independent of motivation. For example, perhaps the original desired action is writing a page each day. The minimum required action, however, is writing two sentences every day, no matter what. Few circumstances provide a legitimate excuse for avoiding this action.

This action may seem trivially small, but it creates positive momentum. The strongest resistance often occurs before starting, when projecting expected states. These projections tend to be far more unpleasant than reality. Starting anyway forces attention away from projections into the task itself. This shift typically allows flow to occur and causes a productive chain reaction. One sentence turns into two, then a paragraph. Before long, a page, which was the real desired action, is written.

Minimum required actions don't always produce massive gains in productivity. Some days produce only a single sentence. That's alright. The beauty of your minimum required action is that progress always occurs. Each small action adds momentum toward larger desired actions while minimizing thoughts like *I did nothing toward my goals today.* With such low execution friction, this tactic almost always increases progress, results, and discipline.

GET SPECIFIC

As discussed previously, high-level aspirations are usually too vague to implement directly. Specific, concrete action steps are far easier to take. Specificity is the difference between I'll work on my book today and I'll write two pages today. The first statement is amorphous and airy. Does writing count? Does editing count? Does reading a blog post about writing count? Vague aspirations make knowing what to do difficult. The second statement contains a clear action with explicit success criteria. It shows exactly what is needed.

Refining your goals into specific actions drastically reduces execution friction. Vague goals require you to decide each day what counts as appropriate and sufficient progress. Making this choice in the moment wastes time and creates indecision: *Do I edit a page? Write a new section? Read another book? Which action step best fulfills my goal?* Without specificity, the decision must be made repeatedly. In the worst case, we make no decision at all and avoid taking action altogether.

Choosing action tools during each event means you're likely to change your tools often, which makes it hard to evaluate effectiveness. In addition, frequent switching means you don't develop expertise with any particular tool. Specifying beforehand narrows your options so you can focus on execution and analysis instead of tool choice. Here are two heuristics for determining if your actions are specific enough. First, you should be able to estimate how long the action takes: "Working on my book" is an indefinite period, but writing two pages can be estimated based on how fast you write. Second, the same result should be expected if the task were hypothetically assigned to someone else. Whether you or I execute it, writing two pages has a clear outcome. Working on a book doesn't.

Here's another example of how specificity reduces decisions and eases execution. Compare, "I will exercise more for a month" to "I will do a home workout three times a week. The workout will be three sets of squats, pushups, and pull-ups to failure." The first example requires many decisions. What kind of workout? How often? Where will you do it? The second example answers all those questions. No wasted energy deciding when or how to exercise. You can focus exclusively on implementing instead.

Let's step through the process of making a nebulous goal more specific: "I want to eat healthier." You start by general tunneling for action steps.

—*How can I eat healthier?*

—Cutting down on sweets would help.

Now you need to tunnel around the frequency.

—How often should I eat sweets?

—At most, once a week.

We've made progress, but there's more refining to be done. What are the metrics for success? Further tunneling is required.

—How long will I do this for?

—How many treats are allowed on that day?

—Is it on a specific day?

—What counts as a sweet?

The process identifies potential decisions and clarifies them now, long before you actually have to make the decision. The more options you eliminate, the clearer and more specific the action becomes.

At this stage, you know exactly how to eat healthier: *For the next month, I won't eat any candy or pastries, except on Sundays. On Sundays, I'll savor up to two, maximum.* This level of specificity is clearly executable and straightforward. It also generates easily analyzable data, which can be used for future adjustments. We'll cover this process in depth later.

Vague goals make you pick action tools haphazardly, hoping they're optimized. It's the equivalent of throwing wood in a pile and nailing pieces together, aspiring to build a shed. The required actions are somewhat known, but co-ordination will be shoddy. Clarity and specificity reduce execution friction and increase follow-through. It allows you to focus on executing your plan instead of expending willpower, making countless decisions about how to act.

LACK OF ACTION IS NOT AN ACTION

Lack of action is not an action you can aspire to take. This may sound ridiculously simple, but it's particularly useful in the context of breaking negative habits. "I want to stop losing my temper" is an admirable aspiration, but what can you actually do about it? Simply saying, you don't want to do something anymore doesn't change your behavior. Luckily, a few tactics can introduce action to goals that don't have associated actions by default.

Alternative Action

Eliminating a negative habit is much easier when a replace-ment action exists. Trying to stop a particular behavior cre-ates instances where relevant decisions become the center of attention. Setting a replacement beforehand eliminates the difficulty of choosing in the moment and provides an alternative place to direct your attention. This makes it eas-ier to dissolve the initial impulse.

Here's an example. Let's say you want to quit smoking. During this process, you will almost definitely feel like smoking occasionally. If you decide beforehand to walk around the block whenever this urge arises, you've provided yourself with a viable alternative path. It may still be difficult to walk that path, but at least you'll know it exists instead of having to fabricate one on the spot.

Alternative actions are also much easier to track and analyze for adjustments: *Is walking around the block appealing enough to curb the urge to smoke? How often does it work? What else can I try?* These are specific, answerable questions. Focusing on lack of action, on the other hand, provides no clues as to future adjustments. Lower the difficulty of making the desired choice by deciding on an alternative long before you make the decision.

Counting Resisted Impulses

Many unwanted behaviors are appealing because they produce immediate gratification, even though the long-term impacts are negative. Combating these impulses is easiest when a viable alternative also produces immediate gratification. This can lead to trading one bad habit for another. In most cases, impulse tracking can be used as a safe alternative to start eliminating undesirable behavior.

Impulse tracking is as simple as it sounds, it only requires keeping a running total of each instance where you resisted an undesirable impulse. For example, let's say the urge to procrastinate arises, but you choose to work through it. Add that to the running total of times you've successfully warded off that impulse. It takes time to build the habit of noticing impulses, but it's a generally useful skill. In addition, counting each success offers a number of benefits.

Many individuals find immediate gratification by adding to their total. Each mark is a tangible sign of success, which builds confidence and esteem. It's also easy to set goals around streaks or other measures of quantity. As streaks grow, most of us become increasingly reluctant to break them. This creates friction, nudging you away from undesirable behavior.

....

Just remember breaking a streak isn't a failure. You simply start again, knowing how well you've done in the past.

....

SET ASIDE TIME

The previous tactics cover how to follow through, but not when to take action. Planning and protecting specific times for taking action eliminates the excuse of I just didn't have time today. Most goals lend themselves to some kind of blocking, allowing wiser allocation of your most valuable resource: time. Time management skills are critical in executing plans efficiently while maintaining balance.

Let's use exercise as an example. You've already decided on cardio three times a week. That's a great start, but when will it happen? Assigning time blocks to the goal increases clarity. Which three days of the week? Monday, Wednesday, Friday. Closer, but it still doesn't have an assigned time block. When during those days? 7 to 8 p.m. You now have a plan for exactly when to take action.

Scheduling blocks makes it easier to protect time from yourself and others. Specific schedules disarm those who attempt to persuade you into other activities: "I always work on my book 5 to 6 p.m. on weekdays" is more convincing than "I wanted to do some work this afternoon." You can also always defer to "I'm busy 5 to 6 p.m. on weekdays" if you don't want to divulge personal details. Other obligations tend to be an excuse people don't take personally. For those susceptible to peer pressure, predetermined blocks provide a gentle option for declining distractions.

Rigid time blocks don't work well for every person and goal. Event triggers can be a useful alternative in situations that require more flexibility. Following event triggers means completing the desired action after another common or scheduled activity. For example, taking a walk immediately after work on Monday, Wednesday, and Friday. The time you leave may vary, but the event chain doesn't. The next action can be taken whether it's noon or midnight. This is especially useful for those with irregular schedules.

Blocking time reduces ambiguity in taking action. With time already allocated, you're more likely to follow through with the scheduled task. Without planning, you may fall prey to moment-by-moment whims, which tend to deprioritize blueprint goals. Blocking also creates timelines that avoid overscheduling or unrealistic expectations. Knowing how you'll spend your time ensures you do so wisely.

AVOID MULTITASKING

We briefly mentioned multitasking while defining happiness, but it's relevant in executing as well. Multitasking, for the purposes of this section, is focusing on multiple tasks in a relatively short period of time (think minutes or hours, not months or years). Switching tasks this quickly is cognitively expensive, with plenty of research backing that claim. Accordingly, efficient efforts require limiting distractions and eliminating multitasking.

While many feel accomplished while multitasking, research shows those are misguided perceptions. Brains can only focus on one event at any given moment. This can be done fast enough that it feels like completing multiple tasks simultaneously, even though mechanically, you're rapidly switching between individual tasks. These switches tax your mental resources. Each focus switch is like slamming a car into reverse at sixty miles per hour. Changing momentum takes time. More frequent switching means more time spent changing direction instead of producing results. Many studies have shown an overwhelming majority of individuals experience a steep decline in both productivity and quality while multitasking.

Multitasking can only be effective with automated tasks that require little or no attention to perform. For example, jogging laps while listening to a podcast. Jogging takes very little cognitive bandwidth, so the information can be focused on without interruption. Even multitasking with automation risks splitting your focus, though. If an unexpected event occurs and demands your attention, like rolling your ankle or running into someone, you'll likely miss all the audio information delivered at that time.

Essentially, unbroken focus increases efficiency. Life may necessitate executing multiple projects each day, but tackling them one at a time is preferable to continuously alternating. Regardless of how productive multitasking may feel, research has repeatedly shown that's not the reality.

ENERGY MANAGEMENT

While not exactly a system tool, it's worth briefly noting that physical states also influence whether you follow through. It's hard to take action when your body doesn't cooperate. The realms which apply to most individuals are fitness, diet, daily energy cycles, and sleep. Other, less common biological factors, like disease, may be relevant on a case-by-case basis as well. In some cases, these concerns must be addressed before you can work on other goals effectively.

For example, consider the following scenario. You can stay awake two hours later to finish writing a paper or wake up two hours earlier. Which option is best? The answer depends on your mindscape. Some individuals work well late into the night, others prefer the morning. Each person has different ebbs and flows of energy throughout the day. Building your schedule around these fluctuations can significantly improve productivity.

A full exploration of physical health is beyond the scope of this book, but I wanted to highlight its impact on other goals. If you're struggling to maintain your energy for taking action, physical health or daily timing is likely the culprit. While health is important, it often falls to the wayside. Investing in even a couple of small improvements, like setting a bedtime, can dramatically improve your energy levels and results.

MEASURING PROGRESS

You're probably sick of hearing this by now, but it's impossible to track progress toward nebulous goals: I want to be wealthy has no endpoint. How do you know when "wealth" has been achieved? Is $100,000 wealthy? $1 million? $50 million? Is making $200 today on track or not? Metrics provide a concrete way of measuring and comparing results. From there, you can analyze your progress and adjust your action tools accordingly.

Metrics should be tied to numbers, a binary yes-no, or some other tangible value. Desired actions are specific enough when they can easily be tracked this way: "Yes, I went to the gym today. I completed one hundred jumping jacks; I spent $345 today. No, it wasn't under my goal of $200; I wrote five pages today." These metrics provide unbiased, accurate reports of actions and/or results, which can be used to assess progress toward higher-level goals.

Collecting data also increases accountability. Data doesn't lie. Many individuals feel increased pressure when creating a record, which in itself can increase motivation. Occasionally, however, tracking creates nervousness: *I'm creating evidence of my shortcomings.* That's a misguided frame. Performance, both good and bad, must be clear to improve and amplify progress. Poor results don't indicate weakness; they're a signal to adjust the approach. Tracking metrics simply helps determine what's actually effective.

TRACK EXTERNALLY

Many are tempted to estimate their progress mentally: *I've mostly been eating healthy; I'm doing well.* This is a mistake. Human memory is highly fallible and only approximates reality. Perceptions may feel accurate, but your brain has finite space. It constantly takes shortcuts to encode and compress only a subset of information. This is practical but leaves plenty of room for error. Perceptions about past actions can easily be incorrect and are an unreliable basis for future adjustments.

Each recollection of an event is created in the context of your current mind. Over time, details can warp around your frames and beliefs. This has been shown in multiple studies, including one where researchers convinced individuals of fake events from their childhood, such as an air balloon trip. These fake memories were created by showing a doctored photo and repeating the story across three instances. Almost half of the participants felt like it was a genuine memory and were able to add additional, obviously fabricated details about the experience.

Here's a personal example to further illustrate memory's fragility. I once committed to a pre-recorded, thirty-day workout program. I followed it diligently, skipping only a day or two in the process. Afterward, I felt stronger and proud of my consistency. That is until I calculated the timeline. It took me 45 days to complete the program, which means I skipped a lot. Worried, I decided to benchmark some new strength metrics against ones I had tracked in the past. Few measures improved, and some actually decreased. The results didn't match my perceptions at all.

I was lucky to have reference points so I could make retroactive calculations. Usually, data must be recorded in the moment or it's lost forever. Relying solely on memory generally creates inaccurate snapshots. External tracking, on the other hand, provides unfaltering evidence. This can be done with minimal effort. There's no need to record every minute detail. Instead, it only requires quickly jotting down data aligned with your key metrics. This is far more reliable than expecting your memory to function perfectly.

ACTION TRACKERS

There are a number of system tools for action tracking. At a minimum, any action tracker should provide a structure for comparing tasks, time, and results. The most common action trackers are spreadsheets and checklists, which prioritize efficiency. Designing them may take longer, but actually entering your data takes only a few seconds: Did I go to the gym today? Yes. These tracking tools are fast and simple, with little friction.

Let's create a spreadsheet-style action tracker to illustrate. First, you write a task in each row. Then you write a timeline across the columns. Your results are then written in the corresponding cell, typically after task completion or at the end of each time period. Each entry should only take a few seconds, though developing the habit of using the tool is a prerequisite.

Recording for two weeks would generate something like this:

Day	Mon	Tue	Wed	Thurs	Fri	Sat	Sun
Week 1							
Pages	1	0	3	1	1	2	0
Gym	Yes	No	No	Yes	No	Yes	Yes
Week 2							
Pages	1	1	2	1	4	2	1
Gym	Yes	Yes	Yes	Yes	No	Yes	No

The resulting table shows exact actions and when they occurred. There's no space for mistaken memory, just numbers and values. You can be confident that your baseline assumptions are correct when analyzing this data for results, patterns, and improvements later.

Action trackers can be further enhanced by social accountability. Completing trackers with someone else can transform administrative overhead into comradery. This can also serve as an additional reminder to actually track the data since someone else is expecting it. If you know anyone who would be interested, consider action tracking in tandem.

JOURNALING

Action trackers produce clear, concise data about goal progress, but they don't capture everything. While it's useful, raw data doesn't record the context of your thoughts, feelings, and experience. This information can produce useful insights that simple action trackers fail to account for. If you can invest the time, journaling is a great tool for creating more robust action tracking information.

Journaling is a fairly ubiquitous idea, so I'll just touch on a few key points. In this context, journaling should specifically be about action taken toward your goals. The most useful data comes from writing (audio or video are viable options as well) your unfiltered experience, letting thoughts flow naturally. These recordings are meant as off-the-cuff explorations, so there's no pressure to craft perfect prose and no reason to edit entries. Just create what comes to you.

Here's an entry on daily writing (taken from my book *Real Resolutions*) as an example:

> Another day where I spent too long staring at a blank page. I'm exhausted and feel like the content is low quality. On days I don't work a shift, writing is much easier. I don't feel rushed or exhausted. When I pick what I want to write about beforehand, the words flow out much more easily. If I don't have a solid topic, it always feels like I've been writing for ages, but my word count doesn't reflect it.

You may have noticed this entry doesn't transition smoothly between topics. It jumps around, mirroring the raw stream of thoughts. The entry is comprehensible, but nowhere near polished. In addition, it's only about a paragraph in length. Even relatively short entries can contain rich context beyond what action trackers provide. If you want more data or feel like creating more, longer entries are always an option.

Journaling's primary benefit is forcing reflection with enough clarity to communicate experiences in words. This process requires investment in thinking about thoughts, feelings, actions, and patterns, thus increasing your meta-cognitive awareness. This awareness shows you more options for optimizing happiness. As a bonus, journaling also produces additional data to lean on during future reflection and analysis.

The downside to journaling is that it can become a significant time investment, especially when spread across many goals. Writing a paragraph each day for ten action tools isn't always feasible. Ideally, action tracking, journaling, or other data-creation tools should be combined to generate information without becoming overwhelming. The goal isn't aimlessly recording everything, it's honing the process for generating useful information.

REVIEWING PROGRESS

Making wise adjustments is far easier after gathering data about your progress. Implementing a regular review process clarifies which tools are effective and which should be adjusted or dropped. Knowing this allows fast iteration with incremental improvements. These adjustments prevent stagnation and usually produce results far better than haphazardly guessing based on perception.

Reviewing your progress can be light and straightforward. For example, scanning results at the end of the month looking for clear patterns. Usually, this is enough to locate a few problems or opportunities. From there, tunneling for solutions and improvements is easy. No hardcore math or algorithms required.

For those willing to invest a little more time, most tracking data can be nicely formatted into graphic representations. This is overkill for many goals, but charts or other graphs can reveal trends that are otherwise hard to see. If you have the skill or interest, creating a rudimentary graphic can provide a new perspective for mining insights.

Here's an example of what the review process looks like. Say you've been tracking your exercise for a month and decide to review. Skimming the data, you notice that you rarely exercise on Fridays. The next step is tunneling into that pattern.

—*What's preventing exercise on that day of the week?*

—*Friday is my designated date night. I usually exercise at night, so it's hard to fit in both.*

The cause has been identified; next is crafting a solution. What change would solve this problem? The answer: *From now on, I'll work out in the morning on Fridays instead of the evening.*

Without producing and reviewing the data, this insight may have been missed. While regularly missing one day a week may not completely derail the goal, it certainly contributes to outcomes. Compounded, these small adjustments make a serious impact on results. Intentionally working through this process produces results far faster and more reliably than relying on intuition alone.

BREAKING ROADBLOCKS

Reviewing progress helps identify problems, but solutions aren't always clear: *How can I get better results? How can I make this easier? I don't know.* Occasionally, you may get stuck trying to overcome a particular obstacle. Roadblocks can be broken down in a number of ways, but we'll focus on two of the most generally successful tactics:

➡ Fresh perspectives
➡ Project cycling

Fresh Perspectives

Getting stuck generally happens because you can only see the situation from a single, focused perspective. It's like looking for the entrance to a building when you can only see the back. The doorway exists, but it can't be seen from that vantage point. The solution only becomes visible after gaining a broader perspective. This section contains a few methods for generating new perspectives.

The first is imagining a friend asking for advice on the same problem: "I'm having trouble writing in my gratitude journal consistently. Have you got any suggestions on how I might do better?" This pushes your perspective externally, providing distance from individual circumstances. Many find this tactic most useful when the scenario is actually written out, substituting another person's name for your own. It may seem silly, but thinking about the advice you'd give others frequently solves the problem for you as well.

Another tactic is imagining receiving advice from your future self who has already completed the goal.

—How was it done?

—I started putting the journal on top of my underwear in the drawer. That meant I had to pick it up to get dressed.

Again, this reframing changes your vantage point, providing new clarity.

The easiest path to a fresh perspective, however, is asking another person. Others are guaranteed to have an outside perspective and see the problem differently. The process is fairly straightforward. Explain your project, the roadblock, and ask for suggestions on solutions similar to tunneling: "How do you think I can do this better? How can I make it easier?"

Spread across multiple individuals, new perspectives and actionable insights are practically guaranteed. Just remember, while generally helpful, all outside advice should be assessed critically and filtered for good contracting. Some advice is better than others, and being able to distinguish the difference is a critical skill. Fresh perspectives don't help if they point in the wrong direction.

Cycle Projects

If you encounter a roadblock that's not budging, another option is temporarily stopping work on that project. This way, blueprint progress can still be made while providing time to reconsider your approach. Cycling a project doesn't mean quitting; it means making space to return later with a refreshed outlook.

Project cycling works best under a few conditions. First, cycles should be timeboxed with a clear timeline for returning to the original project. This ensures the project isn't dropped altogether. Second, the original project should be replaced by a tangentially related one, where possible. This maintains focus in the realm while breaking concentration on the original goal.

For example, someone stuck improving at martial arts might temporarily cycle to yoga or mountain biking for a month. In this case, health and physical mastery are still prioritized but from a different perspective. These new, related experiences have a high probability of unlocking useful insights for progressing in martial arts. Most blueprints contain tangentially related goals that can be used in this way. If not, however, switching realms entirely is a completely viable option. Tangential goals may produce a slight advantage, but creating space to renew your perspective is the real goal here.

Switching projects when you get stuck may feel like a cop-out. Sometimes it is. Other times, however, breaking your attention is necessary to clear your mind and expand constrained approaches. The mind easily becomes stuck in a routine, repeatedly producing the same ineffective solutions. Novelty in other realms helps clear your mental slate. Later, that space can be restocked with new tools that are more likely to be effective.

APPRECIATE VICTORIES

It's worth briefly mentioning that reviewing progress provides an excellent opportunity for homebuilding and motivation. Consider dedicating time during the review process to recognizing effort and celebrating action. Revisit difficult instances where you chose the desired path. Growth, progress, and effort deserve appreciation equal to, if not more than, the results themselves. System tools effective in one realm can typically be transposed onto future projects.

DETERMINING CAPACITY

We've covered system and action tools but still haven't discussed how much to take on at once. Should you try one project? Three? Twenty? How much time and effort should be devoted to mindscaping? How do you determine if you're doing too much or not enough? There's no right answer, but there are a few high-level concepts that can help create balance.

Imagine trying to run a marathon, write a novel, revitalize your marriage, and remodel your kitchen with a three-month deadline. This probably seems unrealistic; each project is huge. All four together, with such a short timeline, is intimidating. It's possible, however, that this is the right set of projects and timeline for someone to undertake. It mostly depends on experience, resources, other time commitments, and impact on happiness.

Let's change the scenario. Imagine the same four tasks asked of someone who has published ten books, runs daily, can afford marriage counseling, and owns a home remodeling business. With previous experience and ample resources, those four goals suddenly seem much more achievable. It's still a difficult set of goals, but someone with that background has a plausible chance of accomplishing it all.

Experience largely determines capacity, increasing in tandem. Experience with sets of action tools, like remodeling a home, drastically decreases the difficulty of achieving related goals. Experience with system tools allows a more effective implementation of those action tools. Goal difficulty is relative to your aspirations and previous experience—more experience executing means a greater ability to execute, as you'd expect.

With enough experience, time eventually becomes the bottleneck. Days only have so many hours, no matter how experienced you are. The individual from the example might only be able to complete those four projects if they commit every waking hour to them. There simply may not be enough time for anything else. Determining capacity requires knowing how much time you can dedicate to projects. Many individuals feel like they're underachieving after overbooking more than it's possible to produce in a given day.

On the other hand, many individuals have a false sense of overbooking. I can't count the number of times I've felt busy all day, yet somehow got nothing done. It's common to not have time for the gym in the same month as finishing two seasons of a mindless show. Without data, time seems to just evaporate. Looking closer, however, reveals how time actually leaks—twenty minutes browsing content, another fifteen minutes reading a blog post, twelve minutes looking over old texts, etc. Small, mindless tasks can collectively eat huge chunks of the day.

You need to know how time is spent so you can determine capacity and allocate your time budget accordingly. This process generally uncovers countless hours of unfulfilling time-sucks. Rescuing this time and replacing it with happiness-optimizing alternatives vastly improves the quality of your life. It also reduces negative thoughts associated with under or overbooking.

The last consideration is the overall impact on happiness. How much do you actually want to take on? How much emotional bandwidth do you have? How much of an increase in happiness do you expect to create? While sacrificing now for more desirable states in the future is often preferable, pushing too hard, especially with low impact, can be overwhelming.

Too much introspection, planning, and control can become constricting and robotic. Improving your life requires balance with actually living life. Overinvesting in improving your life generally produces diminishing returns and, after a certain point, net negative impacts. Your mindscape's composition matters a lot here. Goals and growth are important, but so are appreciating and enjoying life. The time any of us has left in life is an unknown, limited variable.

Balance doesn't mean investing in all realms equally. Starting a business may require working seventy-hour weeks in the beginning. The difference lies in who is undertaking the project. One person may enjoy working that much, as it generates pleasure and purpose. Another individual might feel purposefully satisfied at fifty hours and suffer a decreased quality of life beyond sixty hours. The second individual technically has the capacity, but those hours could be invested elsewhere to better optimize happiness.

One rule of thumb for judging balance is comparing actions against potential regret: *Will I regret taking today off to relax? Will I regret binge-watching this TV show? Will I regret this cheat meal?* These questions are meant to induce genuine reflection about outcomes, not guilt you into action. Sometimes the desirable short-term path is actually the right choice. Using projected regret makes it easier to uncover whether a decision optimizes happiness or is one of the impulses you're trying to rewire.

Determining capacity, in a sense, involves the entire mindscaping process. It's about determining the best overall life while being mindful of trade-offs between choices. It's easy to lose track of what's important in this process and optimize pure productivity. The goal, however, is optimizing happiness, not productivity. If productivity and project completion is weighing heavier than overall happiness, it's time to revisit your priorities.

TOOLS IN PRACTICE: EXAMPLES

At this point, a significant number of execution tools have been explored. To provide a comprehensive view of the execution process, this section includes several end-to-end examples. Each example likely includes more detail than needed to understand the concept. The thought is that individuals will intuit different parts based on their experience, and a granular, encompassing perspective allows everyone to fill in the gaps as needed. Each example differs meaningfully, but feel free to skip ahead if the section starts feeling repetitive.

Imagine you've completed a full self-survey and created a blueprint based on those reflections. The blueprint includes the values of health and relationships. A few goals have been refined from those values: higher-quality sleep, better communication, and improved stress management.

Here's what execution might look like based on this hypothetical blueprint, utilizing tools from previous sections:

QUALITY SLEEP

To enact the value of prioritizing health, your first, highest priority goal is higher-quality sleep. First, you tunnel into the ways better sleep will increase your happiness and why it's a priority. Why is better sleep important? You often waste time lying awake at night, causing exhaustion, irritability, and low productivity the next day. You write all the reasons on a whiteboard in your bedroom, so they're seen often, especially in the morning and at night.

You now need action tools that improve sleep quality. You're not sure of the underlying problem, so you decide to survey your current behavior looking for patterns. You start brainstorming, tunneling around sleep behaviors:

- → When do you usually go to bed?
- → How do you feel when trying to sleep?
- → Are you trying to sleep when you're tired or at a set time?
- → What are you doing before bed?
- → What's the difference between your best and worst nights of sleep?

All the answers are written down. Those answers are used for further tunneling, which is written down as well. After three rounds, patterns come to the surface: *You typically try to sleep between midnight and 4 a.m. You are often looking at screens right before sleeping. Outside lights are disruptive and often present.* These insights seem relevant enough to consider further action.

You then research expert opinions on improving sleep quality to combine with your insights. You research using questions like, *What does good sleep look like? How can I sleep better?* while looking for specific action tools. Searching online confirms your intuitions, as well as uncovering three promising action tools; setting a consistent bedtime, wearing a sleep mask, and stopping electronics use for an hour before bed.

After finalizing action tools, you look at the tactics of social influence and adjusting your environment to make executing your plan easier. You ask your partner for help sticking to an 11 p.m. bedtime. You also attach a note to the bathroom mirror with a sleep mask reminder. Finally, you set your phone to automatically shut down at 10 p.m.

You then create a simple spreadsheet to track actions. It has a column for each day of the week. It also has three rows, one for each action. Each cell correlates to a "yes" or "no" for using the tool on a corresponding day. There's also a fourth row to indicate sleep quality on a scale from 1 to 10. You're now set up to easily track quality and consistency. You start using the tracker the same night it's made. Here are the results after one week:

	Mon	Tue	Wed	Thurs	Fri	Sat	Sun
Mask	Y	Y	Y	N	Y	N	N
Bedtime	N	Y	N	Y	N	N	Y
Phone	Y	N	N	Y	N	Y	Y
Quality	6	3	4	8	2	7	6

You set aside time to reflect on the first week's results. During this time, consider patterns, victories, and potential adjustments. The sleep mask is bothersome—it's been waking you up. Perhaps you're not yet accustomed to it, but you still make a note to consider other options for reducing light. The consistent bedtime and lack of electronic screens seem to increase your sleep quality. You decide to continue without adjustments, focusing on building these habits.

You continue this routine for a few months. Your sleep feels better, the actions are closer to defaults, and the data proves the same. Your average sleep quality increased from five to seven. You automatically stop using your phone at 10 p.m. and are naturally tired by 11 p.m. After three reflection cycles, you replaced the sleep mask with heavy blinds, which has been far more effective. The original sleep problems are essentially gone.

The habits feel more natural now, so you feel comfortable reducing tracking. Daily entries are downgraded to weekly. After several more months, you feel confident these actions are automatic and decide to move forward. You reduce tracking to monthly, freeing most of your time. You're ready to execute another goal.

STRONG COMMUNICATION

Our next blueprint item is improving communication to fulfill the value of relationships. Again, you start by writing down why it's important. Poor communication is eroding valuable relationships, especially with your family. It's also limiting career growth. You set a morning alarm as a reminder to recite this affirmation: "I am working on improving relationships to be closer with family and improve career options." This recitation is followed by a visualization of what success in this realm looks and feels like.

You then survey your current communication style. All you know right now is you're not communicating effectively. To gather additional data, you spend a week tracking your conversations, using your journal to make a note of your experience and outcomes. A few trends emerge: you get frustrated easily, you take it personally when others don't understand your intent, and others seem bored during the conversation.

With a clearer picture, you search for corresponding action tools. You read a highly rated communication skills book for specifics. The book includes several prospective tools, like asking clarifying questions and limiting assumptions. You commit to asking ten clarifying questions and resisting the impulse to make one assumption each day.

You add the reward of a new t-shirt for achieving this for ten consecutive days.

The next day, you start tallying each time you ask a clarifying question or resist the impulse to make an assumption. In the first week, conversations don't seem to improve at all. Wondering if the action tools are ineffective, you check the data. It shows low implementation consistency, averaging one clarifying question per day and catching no assumption impulses. Instead of switching action tools, you look for alternative system tools.

You decide on the visible reminder of writing a small "A" on your hand for "ask." The next week, you average four questions a day and resist two assumption impulses. This is a huge improvement! In addition, conversations feel better. The tools seem to be working. During your next reflection cycle, you make no adjustments, choosing to focus on increasing consistency.

Shortly afterward, an assumption causes a huge, emotionally challenging argument. You reflect on the interaction with homebuilding at the top of your mind. Thoughts like *Maybe I can't communicate well* are reframed as *This interaction did not go the way I wanted and feels bad. I need more experience using communication tools.* You accept negative thoughts and feelings as part of the process instead of trying to fight them. Instead of framing it as a failure, you redirect your thinking toward solutions. You decide to add and track more tools, such as walking away from heated conversations.

Another few weeks pass. You use all the tools and hit your goal targets for ten consecutive days, earning your self-reward. Communication skills still need work, however, so you set a more difficult goal with a corresponding reward. After six months, clarifying questions happen habitually in most interactions. You swap it out for another action tool. Making assumptions is still a problem, but your chosen action tool of tallying resisted impulses doesn't seem to help. You look for another tool to take its place.

A year on, your communication skills are noticeably better. You have progress and results to be proud of. The action tools you've found so far are habitual. You still want to improve your communication skills further, however, so you return to the research phase. New action tools are uncovered, and the process is repeated with new goals.

STRESS MANAGEMENT

The last goal is improving stress management to fulfill the value of health. As you might expect, you first compile the reasons it's important. You decide the most compelling factor is that research has linked stress to decreased lifespan. Beyond this, you often feel exhausted by stress, which causes you to lash out, thus undermining the value of relationships. Combined, these factors are severely limiting your happiness.

You tunnel through your mindscape around these concerns: *What's causing me stress? How do I currently manage my stress? How often is stress overwhelming?* After one round, you clearly recognize the root cause is work deadlines. It always feels like projects are behind schedule. Tunneling into that insight produces the realization that fear of failing on these projects is producing constant stress.

You immediately see several pathways for better managing stress. You can look for stress tools, relaxation tools, productivity tools, work communication tools, or tools that act on fear of failure. After reflection, it seems general stress management tools will be most impactful as they can be utilized in realms other than work.

This is an important goal, and you can afford to commit time and money to it. You decide on a more powerful tool: a week-long immersive stress management course. The course is highly structured and provides a significant number of tools and experience in using them. Afterward, you focus on building habits based on the most effective tools from the program. For additional information and insights, you choose to journal about the process's effectiveness. A few weeks later, it doesn't seem like a good fit. You're using tools consistently but feel equally stressed.

Given your resources, you look for an even more powerful tool and outside expertise. You settle on hiring a personal stress management coach for daily sessions. They share additional tools and insights. After a month of effort, results appear. Work projects seem less daunting. Other activities are less stressful, as well. More effort is required to

achieve the higher-level goal of improving stress management, but a useful path has been identified.

These examples have clearly been simplified for the
sake of brevity. Real life will provide a nuanced mix of
challenges, wins, and defeats along the way. Growing is
usually more complex and less linear. Substantially optimizing your happiness takes serious time and effort, often
including more detours than you'd like or expect along the
way. The point of this section is to roughly explore what execution looks like holistically. Executing efficiently requires
building skills across the strategies and tactics mentioned
in this chapter.

IT'S JUST WHO I AM

There's one last concept that it makes sense to cover here,
with the majority of the framework behind us. A common
roadblock to optimizing happiness is associating with an
identity that inhibits happiness. For example, believing
you are a "stupid person," "pushover," "clingy," or a "'couch
potato." These identities can come from a number of sources such as past traumas, external blueprints, lack of effort,
or believing traits are fixed, just to name a few. Essentially,
everything covered in this book impacts identity and the
attachment to it.

Most individuals associate themselves with a conglom-
eration of stable traits and roles: *I'm an easy-going, curious,
introvert, but I can be lazy. I'm a hard-working, explorative,*

socialite. I'm a mother, student, boxer, etc. These stories generally come attached to a range of self-imposed, expected behaviors. When identity-associated behavior conflicts with optimizing happiness, most individuals side with their identity, blaming the outcome on "It's just who I am."

Identity frames are particularly hard to dissolve because they're so strongly internalized. At the core, however, they're simply labels. These labels are fully malleable, especially in the long term. If you're skeptical, let's explore common social roles. How would you act in the roles of teacher, babysitter, friend, or student? Most people would admit each produces slightly different behaviors. Yet, one individual is fully capable of being a teacher, babysitter, friend, and student.

Behavior expectations are tied directly to the strongest identity at that moment: *I'm a mother now. I can't be irresponsible.* The role dictates which actions are correct, significantly reducing friction toward those actions. The label alone, however, has no impact whatsoever. You force these behaviors on yourself after internally identifying with the title.

While roles may change little in a given day, they change drastically over time. The musician from high school becomes an athlete and vice versa. The reckless party animal becomes a quiet, stable parent, and so on. Not everyone changes drastically, but everyone is capable of undertaking a new identity. It happens naturally for many individuals as they age and grow.

Consider the person you were five years ago. Now ten. Now fifteen. How alike are those versions of yourself? Would they agree on every part of their identities? Unlikely. These changes are the result of small thoughts and actions slowly shifting and rebuilding your identity behind the scenes.

By explicitly controlling your personal narrative, this process can be hijacked. You can choose roles in alignment with desired behaviors. This is the difference between *I'm a nonsmoker,* and *I'm a smoker who's trying to quit.* While this adjustment may seem trite, the identities you internalize have massive impacts on how executing feels. This, in turn, drastically affects actions and outcomes.

Intentionally guiding this process takes time and coordination. Multiple levers must work together to create happiness-optimized identity-level shifts. The first step is tunneling to understand how the identities you choose to identify with are influencing your life. You need to dismantle counterproductive associations before you can truly optimize happiness.

....

It can be hard to break the spell, but
you choose the stories you tell yourself.
If identity can change by chance,
it can also change by choice.

....

EXAMINING HOW OTHERS EXECUTE

Everyone has the option of choosing more or less desirable pathways. Not everyone knows the tools for determining the difference and acting on them consistently. Gaps between wanting to achieve a goal and knowing how to do it are common. The concepts in this chapter allow more empathy for those struggling to execute consistently. How can they achieve more if they've never been exposed to effective strategies and tactics for executing?

DO THEY HAVE THE RIGHT TOOLS?

"I'm starting a new diet this week. I'm going to lose 20 lbs!" It's a statement heard countless times from a parent, co-worker, best friend, or whoever else. It's not definitely a lost cause, but it didn't happen the last twenty times they said it either. You want to be supportive, but having faith is hard given their past record.

Let's re-examine the scenario in the context of pathway resistance, skill tools, and system tools. Do they know how to increase resistance to undesirable actions? Lower resistance to desirable actions? Are they using the right action tools? Are they familiar with system tools? Do they have clear metrics for success? Are they tracking progress? "No" is a common answer for most, if not all, of these questions.

Individuals without execution knowledge are likely to encounter a number of roadblocks in achieving goals. Maybe they don't know which actions achieve their goals.

Maybe they do but can't execute consistently. Perhaps they perceive consistency and results but aren't tracking data, which would prove otherwise. Maybe they're progressing but using slow, inefficient tools which take ten times longer. Any combination of these factors will significantly hinder their progress.

Most people haven't been exposed to, let alone learned and practiced, tactics for overcoming these roadblocks. They only utilize one or two of these levers, if they use any at all. This creates high-resistance paths occasionally traveled through agonizingly high effort and sheer willpower. Results tend to be discouraging and unreliable. When stalled, those around them often become bad contractors, generating further resistance. Improving results requires exposure to tools and frames which solve these problems.

In addition, most individuals are unfamiliar with value-goal branching techniques, seeing only a handful of routes to fulfillment. These severely limit the person's creativity and chances of success. Imagine wanting to improve your physical health but thinking pushups are the only exercise. Progress would be difficult and partial, neglecting major muscle groups. Individuals must understand the broader ecosystem to execute effectively. Most don't, making it easier to empathize with a lack of progress. They're trying to build a wall when the only known tool is a pickaxe.

Beyond increasing empathy, adopting this frame provides ample opportunities to create low-cost wins for others. When others struggle to take action, you can expose them to relevant high-level concepts, share specific system and skill tools, or actually help them to execute. For example, explaining how to create the path of least resistance, helping create an action tracker, or tunneling through blockage points with them. Sharing your expertise in overcoming common roadblocks can drastically improve their results.

Sharing should only be done if others actually want the advice. Overbearingly interjecting is unlikely to work well. When solicited, exposure to these concepts is likely to improve results, but don't forget the importance of fitting tools to each mindscape. Tools that work for you may not work for them. Sharing may include specific tools, but providing guidance around the process itself tends to produce the best results. This allows them to experiment and customize based on their experience and unique mindscape.

PLANS ARE WORTHLESS WITHOUT ACTION

Blueprints are only enacted through action. Most individuals make plans but struggle to execute consistently and effectively. Accordingly, we spent the bulk of this chapter discussing a wide number of action and system tools for overcoming this problem.

Mastering these tools allows for the successful implementation of blueprint components. Want to become a better speaker? Run it through the process. Want to be kinder? Run it through the process. Regardless of the aspiration, you can apply this process and expect results over time. The importance of execution cannot be overemphasized.

At this point, we have covered reflecting, planning, and executing. This is, more or less, the cycle used to shape mindscapes and fully optimize your happiness. There are, however, a few supplemental ideas that keep the process running smoothly: general maintenance and natural disasters.

REFLECTION

The following set of questions is designed to help distill the ideas in this chapter. Take your time answering them and revisit any practices or exercises if you need to.

- → What goals are you working on this week?

- → What habits are you working on right now?

- → When was the last time you completed a goal?

- → How many action tools do you typically try before giving up on a project?

- → What system tools do you use regularly?

- → How well do you track your goals?

- → Who can help you achieve your goals?

- Who can help you change your habits?

- What's the last new system or action tool you tried?

- How often do you ask others for help with habits or goals?

- How have you made desired habits the path of least resistance?

- How motivated are you to execute your goals and habits?

- How often do you schedule and protect time for projects?

- How do you analyze data for projects?

- How do you measure progress on your projects?

- What adjustments have you made to a current goal?

- How do you create an environment for success?

- What most often slows down your execution?

- How often do you procrastinate?

- How consistent are you in taking action?

7

GENERAL MAINTENANCE

General maintenance touches the few topics relevant to mindscaping, which fall slightly outside the previous chapters. It deals with habits, landscape feature decay, and blueprint audits. This is mostly review, tying up loose ends without introducing many new or difficult concepts.

MOVING HABITS TO MAINTENANCE

The last chapter focused exclusively on goals because they can be used to build corresponding habits. Yet, habits, by definition, don't have an endpoint. How can you determine when you've actually built the habit? When can you shift focus away from developing the habit of being nice toward waking up early? You need an endpoint to determine capacity and project planning.

The best indicator of how much investment a habit requires is how automatic it has become. How often is the desired action the default when no additional effort or focus is applied? While this question shows how much effort is necessary, it's hard to answer. You can't be sure a habit is automatic without tracking, which adds effort and focus to the task. In these cases, an approximation is the most viable option. Track the action, but pay attention to how hard making each decision is.

Here's an example to illustrate. Your aspiration is healthy eating habits. To start, this habit is too nebulous. It must be more specific to gauge success toward automation. Instead, let's specify replacing cereal with a healthier breakfast. For your entire life, sugary cereal has been the norm. You start the day, pour a bowl, and eat it without thinking. Currently, that's the automatic behavior you want to swap for a healthier one.

Eating fruit for breakfast seems like a better choice. In the beginning, this will demand high effort. Years of cereal eating need to be unwound and replaced. This requires actively remembering the goal and making decisions: *Do I want a banana or apple for breakfast?* Even with great system tools, new habits require the most willpower upfront.

This new habit can be supported with the goal of eating fruit for breakfast every day for three months, and tracking accordingly. The real goal, however, is shifting the default. After achieving the three-month goal, results should be reviewed for difficulty. If it's still difficult, consider whether the method needs adjustment or if you simply need more repetitions. Then start the process again. It may take a few cycles, but eventually, choosing fruit for breakfast will become the easier default choice.

There are no concrete rules for when to actually switch. It's more of a gut feeling for when eating fruit seems more natural than sugary cereals. At a minimum, the desired habit should feel low cost, automatic, and unimportant, relative to other options. Then you can consider reducing tracking and converting the habit from active investment to passive maintenance.

SCALE BACK SLOWLY

Habit change is meant to endure the long term. One of the most common roadblocks to this is thinking it's become automatic too early. Habits can seem set in stone when they've simply become easier. Switching too early in the process will cause gradual reversion. Tracking habits for a longer period than seems necessary ensures this doesn't happen. Tracking doesn't need to be done at the same intensity for the entire time, though. That's too much overhead. Instead, as successful subgoals mount, tracking efforts can be reduced accordingly.

There's no consensus about exactly how long solidifying a habit takes. Most estimates are in the ballpark of two to six months. These numbers may generally work, but in some instances, new habits will slowly decay and revert, even after six months. Having a good couple of months and then reverting to the starting point six months later happens to many people. Tracking at increasingly spaced intervals keeps overhead low but monitors consistency for hiccups.

A rough minimum guideline for tracking reduction is executing your habit more than 80% of the time (however you define that) for at least two months. Two months is the lower-end estimate of how long solidifying a habit takes. Missing 20% or more is too often to be considered a default. This minimum may seem high in some cases, but it's far better than the risk of progress reverting.

After hitting the minimum level, tracking frequency can be reduced. For example, daily sleep tracking could be reduced to biweekly entries. The minimum consistency threshold is then reset. If your results stay consistent, tracking can be further reduced to once a week. Rinse and repeat until tracking no longer seems necessary. The goal is to generate just enough data to be aware of whether or not the habit is slipping.

Reduced tracking is most accurate when using randomized checks. This means checking during completely arbitrary dates or times instead of every Monday or Wednesday at noon. For example, you would randomly pick four dates to check. Let's say the 5th, 14th, 18th, and 27th. Then set a reminder to gauge habit execution on those dates. Randomizing avoids cheating by putting extra effort in on days you expect checks. Habits should be built to stick generally, not just on preset, regular checking intervals.

Reduction rates are up to you, but six months to a year are rough guidelines for validating change. This may seem lengthy, but tracking can be reduced as you go. Keeping occasional checks allows you to be confident you're maintaining progress over time.

WHAT IF IT NEVER BECOMES AUTOMATIC?

What if the habit you've chosen never feels fully automatic? Some actions require energy and effort regardless of repetitions, even if the choice becomes easier over time. Generally, these are actions that sacrifice current desirable states for future ones, instead of simply transferring between equally agreeable decisions. How should these cases be handled?

Let's take, for example, the habit of always pushing through fear to take action. This action will become easier over time, but by its very nature always requires effort. Acknowledging and overcoming fear requires effort. The default will always be inaction because that's far easier than pushing yourself through an uncomfortable emotion. In these cases, the aim is automating the execution process, instead of the action itself.

Take writing, for example. If you're anything like me, individual moments of writing can be painfully difficult, regardless of frequency or experience level. Each topic and even each sentence requires mental effort. The words never come out on autopilot; they demand attention and effort.

Even though the action isn't automatic or effortless, the process for writing and tracking results can be.

A daily work log with targets and outcomes works for me. Specific projects vary daily, but filling out the log has become automatic. I've done variations of this technique for years now. At this point, there's far more mental resistance in leaving the log blank than filling it out. This habit pushes me to execute most days. The process is automatic, even if the individual actions are not.

Exercise is an example of another habit that can't be fully automated. The individual actions of increasing fitness require effort. What can be built, however, is a habit of showing up at a gym, class, or time block otherwise dedicated to exercising. This won't guarantee effort and progress, but simply being in the right place helps a lot. It creates the right environment for taking action, even if it doesn't ease the action itself.

For these habits, supporting system tools require less investment over time, while skill tools level off at a certain point. This most often applies to life-long health, education, or skill-building practices, where no ceiling exists. While technically, these habits could be executed so that investment continually decreases, results would also suffer. Generally, that's not the goal, nor is it the path to optimizing happiness.

LANDSCAPE EROSION

Imagine building a fence around your property. The project takes a year, but your fence is beautiful, stable, and sturdy. You move on to other, more pressing concerns. A few years pass. One day you notice how much the fence has deteriorated. It's standing, but weeds are poking through. Panels are broken out. The paint is chipped and faded.

Mindscapes work similarly. As you move through life and change projects, those left unattended are susceptible to erosion. This should be expected, to some degree. Much of what was important five or ten years ago may not be now. There are cases, however, where you may want to revitalize an old habit.

The good news is your fence still exists. It doesn't need to be rebuilt from scratch. Eroded mindscape features tend to work similarly. Pathways built from previous efforts have already been paved, though they may need rehabilitation. The longer they've been unused, the more decay you'll find, but some portion of those tools and experiences are bound to carry forward. Since there's some baseline, reimplementing is far easier than the original undertaking.

Since old habits are usually easier to execute, they're often high impact relative to their cost. This is only true, however, if they're still relevant for optimizing happiness. If an old habit has lost its place in your life, there's no reason to revive it. On the other hand, these projects are often far easier and more fruitful than other undertakings. It's worth weighing out before committing.

PRIORITIZING OLD PROJECTS

We've wandered into yet another prioritization problem. How should the opportunity cost of maintaining old habits be compared against executing current blueprint components? While old habits may be efficient, spending substantial time on maintenance will stall your progress. Which one is better overall?

We discussed multiple methods for prioritization in the blueprint section. These options were meant for those with minimal execution experience. When deciding between past habits and present blueprint goals, it's reasonable to assume more experience with the process. At that point, prioritizing by impact is far more logical, as it will most improve your life. Accordingly, decisions should be based on the ratio of cost to reward. This idea is simple, but actually deciding can be difficult.

One helpful tactic is cost-impact weighing. While highly subjective, this exercise attempts to quantify effort relative to reward. To start, list each potential project. Then, assign each option a value between one and five for expected impact (low impact = 1, high impact = 5) and speed (slow = 1, fast = 5). After estimating values for each habit, multiply the numbers together. The generic formula is Impact x Speed = Value. The results should look something like this:

Diet: 2x3 = 6

Flossing: 5x3 = 15

Jogging: 4x3 = 12

Public Speaking: 3x3 = 9

Ordering this list creates a ranking for the relative value of each project. Higher numbers are more efficient and should be prioritized. Let's look closer at flossing and diet as examples. We'll say flossing is easily and quickly implemented, so it's a five. Your gums have also been bothering you lately, which this is likely to fix, so the impact is a three. Overall, it gets a score of fifteen.

Diet, on the other hand, is estimated to take substantial time and effort to change. You give it a two for speed. On the bright side, food-related health has never been a problem. What you currently eat isn't perfect, but you generally feel good. Your bloodwork always comes back healthy. You decide it has an impact of three. Overall, it gets a score of six.

According to the results, flossing should be prioritized. It has the highest payoffs relative to cost. This exercise gives simple numeric values, but it clearly produces only a rough and fairly arbitrary heuristic. You should consider the full context and implications of each project before moving forward. However, weighing relative rewards can make it much easier to decide what to tackle next.

INTERMITTENT BLUEPRINT AUDITS

Blueprints almost always change over time because life changes over time. Iteration was mentioned several times throughout the book, but only in the barest sense. This topic is worth revisiting briefly with the full framework in retrospect. While blueprint audits can be time-consuming, regularly scheduling them generates continual refinement and makes keeping pace with life's inevitable changes a bit easier.

As blueprints are executed against reality, two experiences typically arise. First, assumptions about which actions optimize happiness turn out to be incomplete. For example, meeting more people to fulfill the value of connection, only to realize deep relationships and connecting with family every week is more fitting. Or perhaps investing time into creating a higher income to achieve stability, but at too high a cost to health. These realizations only come after taking action.

The second experience is feeling how different actions optimize happiness differently across time. This year, charity work achieves your value of contribution, but five years from now, it's replaced by raising children, or exploration becomes a more salient value. Just because an action has optimized your happiness over one time period doesn't mean it will do so forever.

These experiences of refinement and change are fairly universal, so expect to encounter them at some point. Strategic planning helps, but projections are never perfect. Mistakes happen—life changes. Human brains are wired for survival, not happiness, so it's constantly elusive. Accordingly, blueprint updates should be incorporated into the process.

Regular blueprint audits allow adjustments based on experience while reducing the negative impacts of change. Tuning into the high-level process keeps the strategy sane, which is far more important than individual tactics. It may seem like this would happen naturally, but without dedicated time, these reviews can easily be neglected for long periods. Accordingly, it's prudent to plan quarterly, bi-annual, or yearly audits. These frequencies reduce the odds of entirely rewriting your blueprint, making occasional updates instead.

Enacting a blueprint audit is fairly straightforward. Start by tunneling through this question: How well does my blueprint optimize happiness? After answering at the highest level, more specificity can be introduced. Most find checking at the individual value and goal level useful: How does each blueprint value create more desirable states and evaluations? This should be easy to answer. If not, it's a sign that you should re-evaluate.

Second: How well are your current goals fulfilling these values? Has a rotating schedule for calling friends increased connection? Has writing fulfilled the value of being a creator? Are these goals and associated actions producing more desirable states and evaluations? If not, they should be replaced with ones more fitting to your mindscape, or more tightly coupled to a value.

Here's a more tangible example. Say you start running to fulfill the value of being healthy. During an audit, you might tunnel around the question: How well is running increasing your health? Let's say benefits are sparse, it's unpleasant, and it's often causing sprained ankles and joint pain. It doesn't seem like running is increasing your health very effectively.

For most people, running typically fulfills the value of being healthy, but it's not optimizing happiness in this case. That particular action tool is a poor fit for this mindscape because there are plenty of other pathways to being healthy. Auditing on a set schedule provides space to catch and fix these kinds of mismatches at a higher, more strategic level than regular action tracking analysis.

....

It's worth stepping back to evaluate
your overall strategy occasionally.

....

YOU CAN CONTROL THE PROCESS

So, this process never ends? I don't even want to start. It's too controlled and mechanical, plus there's a ton of overhead. I'd rather just live and see what happens. This book is densely packed with concepts, tools, and strategies. Ingesting and implementing it all at once can feel overwhelming. Mindscaping, however, will occur regardless. The choice isn't between using the framework or not; it's between taking control of the process or leaving it to chance.

Every action, whether intentional or not, wires your brain. Features are built and habits form. Environments create nudges. Most people let chance dictate their fate, leveraging only a small percentage of what's controllable. But this means leaving your happiness to luck, circumstance, and random events. With such unstable foundations, results will generally be poor. Haphazardly stumbling into sustainable happiness is rare.

Deliberately guiding your mind's development shifts the odds in your favor. It provides opportunities and confidence to move toward your best life. While constant pleasurable states are unrealistic, the ratio can be still be shifted toward desirability. It's not perfect, but it's far better than the alternative.

Consider the cumulative impact of intentional mindscaping over many years, even with minimal effort. How much happier could you be after ten years of gradual optimization? What about twenty? Or thirty? Just as with a real landscape, working on a mindscape year after year eventually produces breathtaking results. No single project needs to be massive; small changes accumulate over time to drastically improve the baseline.

I'll stop selling so hard, but I genuinely think there's an opportunity here. So many in the world are struggling, experiencing highly undesirable states almost constantly.

Better options exist. Mindscaping need not consume your life, but please consider implementing some version of it, personalized to your tastes. Meaningful improvement can happen. The timeline may be daunting, but quality of life is too important to leave to chance.

REFLECTION

The following set of questions is designed to help distill the ideas in this chapter. Take your time answering them and revisit any practices or exercises if you need to.

➔ Which habits feel automatic?

➔ How much time are you spending tracking? Is it worthwhile?

➔ Could you track any habits less often?

➔ Do you have any habits that won't become automatic? How do you plan to stick with them?

➔ Are there any habits you had three years ago that you want now?

➔ When was your last blueprint audit?

➔ Should any of your old projects be refreshed?

➔ How would you rate current projects on impact and speed?

8

NATURAL DISASTERS – DESTABILIZING LIFE EVENTS

Imagine living in a beautiful estate. It contains a mansion, an expansive lake, and an immaculate garden. A lush forest dotted with walking paths and biking trails surrounds the property. It's everything you could ever hope for, perfectly maintained. Life couldn't be any better.

One day you notice dark clouds off in the distance. As they approach, it becomes clear they're attached to a massive storm. A tornado can be made out in the distance. It's headed right for you. You hurriedly dive into the cellar for safety. Before long, the storm is upon you. Awful sounds rage outside. You can hear trees being torn from the ground, the mansion being ripped apart piece by piece. After a few hours, the storm finally ends. You peek out at the new landscape.

It's an ugly scene. Your marvelous home has been completely leveled. Bits of rubble, glass, and plastering are strewn across the lawn. Huge swaths of the forest are disrupted, hundreds of trees torn from the ground. The lake is practically empty, with other areas flooded. Everything is mangled beyond recognition, a hollow shell of what it was only hours before.

This landscape took years, even decades, to build. It was destroyed in a matter of minutes. Shock barely holds back overwhelming frustration. Then questions arise: *Why? Why me? Why was everything taken from me? All that wasted time. What was the point of building it all? My life is ruined.*

Discussions about mindscaping so far have assumed a relatively stable life, but that's not always the case. Unexpected, devastating incidents happen. Events like death, divorce, illness, and job loss force massive mindscape shifts. These highly stressful events can be absolutely devastating, rendering blueprints obsolete and destroying homes. These changes are irreversible. Returning to the previous state isn't possible; you can only build atop the ruins.

This may sound dramatic, but it would be naive to say you simply discover desirable states, incrementally work toward them, and live happily ever after. Life doesn't work that way, and saying otherwise would be misleading. Unexpected tragedies happen on their own schedule. In most cases, you're powerless to prevent these events. What is in your control, however, is looking for ways to mitigate damage and work toward recovery.

Each natural disaster is unique, requiring different tools to rebuild. As with goal execution, covering every useful action tool is infeasible. Instead, we'll discuss general strategies for dealing with natural disasters. This is a simple primer to help you prepare. Facing an actual disaster requires far more support than the next few pages can provide.

STARTING OVER

Severely life-altering events can crack, if not completely shatter, the foundations of identity. How does one move forward when most goals and past experiences no longer fit? What does the paralyzed Olympian look forward to? The spouse widowed after thirty years? The refugee exiled from their homeland? What are the next steps when a person is forced to start their life over?

These questions are hard to answer, especially right after the event. No simple or straightforward answers exist. Still, there are always pathways to optimizing happiness, even if they're difficult to see during a crisis. Moving forward generally requires completely rebuilding your life and blueprint to accommodate the new circumstances, leaving everything else behind.

This is, of course, far easier said than done. Natural disasters close previously desirable pathways and render many habits ineffective. At the same time, new challenges are introduced in droves. For example, perhaps your significant other handled finances for the last forty years. Now it's your responsibility. Time after work is now empty, since being home for dinner is no longer necessary. The many features impacted by natural disasters are difficult to re-build simultaneously.

Beyond habits, self-esteem and confidence are often assaulted as well. Proud accomplishments may no longer seem meaningful in the new context. Seeing your value may be harder without the places or people you're accustomed to. These drastic changes make it harder to believe in your ability to optimize. Loss can make rebuilding feel futile.

Yet, when all factors are considered, taking action is still the only plausible option. It may be hard, but the alternative is wallowing in pain. Simply sitting still will not create a brighter future or better experiences. Life may deal an unfair hand, but wishing or saying, "This shouldn't be," doesn't change reality. The healing process is never fast or easy, but every effort and step forward counts. It's the only way change happens. While each disaster is unique, here are a few ideas for framing and working through these experiences.

FACE YOUR EMOTIONS

Natural disasters are typically followed by a flurry of unpleasant emotions, like discomfort, frustration, anger, depression, and anxiety. Many of us respond by trying to bury, fight, or ignore these emotions. It's easy to believe this is a form of positive thinking or optimizing pleasure by avoiding discomfort. While logical, these intuitions are misguided and can actually make the problem worse. Emotions must be faced head-on, accepted, and managed appropriately.

When facing such powerful negative emotions, the most common response is burying them with easily achievable but unreliable or costly pleasurable states. Without tools to work through these emotions, most turn to familiar options. It's unsurprising that mind-altering substances, countless hours of video games, binge eating, and other overall net-negative choices are most desirable during hard times. They're reliable ways to create immediately pleasurable states during uncertainty and pain.

The benefits of these choices are short-lived, with each creating happiness debt. Yes, they allow escape from pain momentarily, but they fail to resolve the root cause. The pain will return, prompting another short-term choice. Without intervention, this can quickly devolve into immense pain and reliance on a handful of dangerous tools. With each use, more debt is created, the choice becomes more default, and the problem remains unresolved. This can become a self-fueling downward spiral with horrible consequences.

It's like building a new home atop the ruins of your old home without clearing the rubble. The new foundation is inherently unstable. As more is built upon this foundation, it becomes increasingly unstable. Eventually, it teeters on the brink of collapse. At that point, it's only a matter of time before the entire structure collapses and all debt must be repaid. When the option exists, you should try to break this cycle as quickly as possible.

Some individuals are generally skilled at burying and controlling their emotions. This might work for trivial events like getting cut off in traffic. Anger at traffic doesn't serve any meaningful purpose. Displeasure doesn't influence anyone's driving, and there's nothing to learn from the experience. For this scenario, the anger can be dissipated in a number of ways, including simply changing focus.

Burying emotions is far less effective when it comes to serious traumas. Instead of being stuck in traffic, imagine going blind. This changes your entire life. The emotions involved are higher intensity, serve a purpose, and must be dissected more mindfully. Moving through the experience requires perseverance, acceptance, and patience: *Where are these emotions coming from? What signal is my mind trying to send? How can these feelings help me in the future? How can I accept what has happened?* There's a lot to learn and process.

Feeling pain during trauma is a signal from your mind, even if that signal's purpose is unrecognizable in the moment. For example, grief at the loss of a loved one is a sign of the person's importance. It's a reminder to value life and to prioritize quality time. During a disaster, it may take many hours, weeks, or months of exploring emotions to decipher how the event fits into your life. Keep trying.

This process is never easy, but it's the only way to work through natural disasters. The intensely undesirable states associated with recovery are generally unavoidable. The hard work of clearing debris must happen before rebuilding can start.

....

Finding a way to work with and through emotions instead of circumventing them is critical; otherwise, underlying issues will eat away at your happiness forever.

....

REWORK YOUR BLUEPRINT

Natural disasters are destructive, rendering large chunks of your blueprint obsolete. Creating a blueprint is generally hard at the best of times, but doing so in the midst of chaos, pain, and change requires a herculean effort. On the bright side, there are infinite options for adapting a blueprint. No set of events, no matter how awful, can stop you from optimizing your happiness. States and evaluations can always be worked on for the better.

This is much harder to see and believe in the midst of recovering. Change at this intensity tends to cloud strategic thinking. The good news is blueprints can be iterative. Solving it all at once isn't required. Instead, you can look for any step forward that feels reasonable and feasible. Rebuilding may be the only option, but there's no rush, and it doesn't have to be perfect.

After a disaster, your new blueprint can be simple. In many cases, a blueprint containing only basic self-care is sufficient. Are you safe? Eating? Sleeping? Socializing? Have a place to stay? Disasters tend to remove even the necessities of life so recovering them is essential. These have a big impact on happiness and are also an essential foundation for any future projects.

After your core needs are met, a home inspection is in order. Natural disasters often level homes and with them a belief in our ability, worth, or future progress. These are all required to build a new, sustainable mindscape. All the tactics we covered earlier still apply, though they may need to be applied more delicately than usual.

When your home feels stable, you're well on the way to creating a new blueprint. At this point, revisiting your self-survey and creating a blueprint should be of use. It's not an easy process by any means, but with enough effort and resilience, eventually, a meaningful vision will come together. There's no pressure to quickly produce another blueprint, as these are the most challenging times in life. Do what you can with where you are.

REACH OUT FOR POWERFUL TOOLS

Imagine using only your hands to rebuild after a hurricane. It would take countless years, and most would soon quit. The task is too hard with such a weak tool. When real hurricanes occur, you use the strongest tools available. You pay experts, ask for help from loved ones, and invest in heavy machinery. During destabilizing life events, you should treat your mind similarly and leverage the most powerful resources available.

We spoke earlier about mapping tool strength based on needs. Needs are highest during natural disasters. Every available, applicable tool should be utilized. Tragedies are harrowing experiences, but unfortunately they are rarely entirely unique. Since that's the case, resources exist for most types of natural disasters. Common tools are forms of therapy, support groups, retreats, or coaching, though others exist as well.

Powerful tools are generally costly, but this isn't always the case. Free or inexpensive options like charities or social services exist, particularly for those facing hardships. Research your options extensively, and don't be afraid to ask for help when you find something promising. The altruistic individuals who create these resources derive purpose from serving. They want to do it. Use that kindness to find stability.

In addition, disasters call for the full support of your network. Reach out for help where you can. Let people help when they can. Trying to recover alone hurts you and does them no favors. At the very least, let them help find tools for the situation. Those with a strong sense of pride may find this unnatural, but it's how close relationships work. People help each other during difficult times.

Refusing or not asking for help doesn't make it easier for everyone else, only harder on yourself. Accepting external assistance is often the difference between a full recovery and a downward spiral. Being vulnerable may not be easy, but it's often the only viable long-term option.

....

Natural disasters require the strongest possible tools.

....

CHANGE IS INEVITABLE: SMALL DISASTERS

This chapter has mostly covered massive landscape-shifting events, but small, unexpected events can be impactful as well, just to a lesser degree. Any unexpected event can force blueprints, habits, or goals to evolve. All change generates difficulty and discomfort. These hardships can be moderated by learning to adjust to inevitable changes.

Here's an example. Let's say you exercise consistently. One day the gym shuts down permanently. The closest gym is now an hour away. Your previous habit, as it was constructed, is no longer relevant. This change forces you to change, as well.

An outpouring of negative emotions is a common reaction to this sort of change: *Wow, that's annoying. I can't ex-*

ercise now. How could they do this to me? This is unfair. Venting these frustrations feels good momentarily. It doesn't, however, solve the problem. Optimizing happiness requires transitioning your focus toward solutions.

Tunneling through the emotions is a good first step: What is this emotion telling me? What is the signal here? Tunneling for solutions comes next: How can I solve this problem? How can I optimize happiness in this new scenario? Reasonable options for the example include planning the best way to get to the other gym or finding an alternative form of exercise. Solutions may need adjustment over time, but it's preferable to perpetually lamenting or abandoning the habit.

There's enough in this book about finding alternate pathways; the main point is reframing is often the best option for digesting change. Alterations are never easy, but expecting and accepting them helps. Embracing the inevitability of disruptions frees up your focus for navigating the new terrain. This may sound like a minor frame adjustment, but it's an important one. You can only work on what's in your control. The less time and energy you spend fighting change, the quicker the given reality can be optimized.

DISASTER PREPARATION

On the surface, expecting unexpected change is nonsensical. How can you prepare for disasters without knowing what they are or when they'll arrive? The future can't be predicted, but you can create a solid, resilient foundation. This can be done by homebuilding and diversifying sources of happiness. Knowing when disasters will strike is impossible, but you can prepare to minimize their impact.

How homebuilding helps is fairly straightforward. Would you rather be in a reinforced underground bunker or a small haphazard shack during a tornado? Strong homes weather disasters better. High fortitude protects you from inner turmoil during unexpected events. You must be able to trust yourself to figure out a solution, regardless of the situation. Fortitude also clarifies what's in control, so energy can be expended appropriately.

DIVERSIFY SOURCES OF HAPPINESS

While we've covered homebuilding extensively, diversifying sources of happiness hasn't been covered yet. Most individuals derive the majority of their desirable states from a handful of sources. This creates vulnerability to disasters. If one or more sources are destroyed or blocked, no viable backups exist. As with wealth, diversifying happiness reduces risk.

Diversifying happiness doesn't mean equal investment in hundreds of projects. Spreading energy across too many realms makes giving a full effort or prioritizing impossible. Diversifying doesn't require reducing investment in important and impactful projects. Instead, it means preemptively identifying alternate pathways to desirable states. You only need to know what these options are and give them a little exploration, which doesn't require much investment.

Here's an example. Let's say your blueprint dictates heavy career investment, which comes at some cost to your relationships and health. Assuming trade-offs are clear and happiness is optimized, there's nothing intrinsically wrong with this decision. Investing so heavily in limited realms, projects, or values does, however, create vulnerability. What if an external event blocks that path? Perhaps an honest mistake blacklists you from the industry, preventing all future work in the field. Now what?

It's much harder to pivot if options haven't been explored beforehand. Considering the value in exploring friendships, hobbies, health, or other values makes transitioning slightly less painful. Become familiar with alternative ways of rebuilding your happiness. With preparation, primary sources of happiness become luxuries instead of necessities: *My career in this field is over, but I always wanted to try to dance. Now I have time.*

Feeling like your entire identity can be encapsulated in a single sentence, especially if it's not a value, is a warning sign that more pathways should be developed. If you can't imagine yourself in any situation other than the present one, then your happiness is vulnerable. This doesn't necessarily require direct changes to fix. It does, however, require carving out time to reflect on alternate pathways in case they become necessary later.

This can easily be done by planting low-cost, high-return seeds in other realms. For example, spend a few hours sketching out backup plans; dedicate one day a month to painting instead of your thesis; spend time with friends and family instead of training; or push to your limits at work instead of enjoying your usual leisure time. The specifics don't matter. It's about investing small amounts of time into understanding all the options life has to offer.

These small investments make tunneling after disasters far easier. How can you handle sources of happiness disappearing? What else can you explore? How else can you create desirable states? Diversification provides some ideas and experiences with the answers: *If the Olympics don't work out, starting a food truck might be interesting.*

It may seem like this exercise can be used when needed, but it will be far more difficult by then. Natural disasters cause an overwhelming number of problems. Work done upfront eases intensity during the event. Knowing alternate pathways beforehand frees up resources, allowing you to work through other concerns. This doesn't make the change itself easier but does streamline transitioning into the next steps.

However, even with a good foundation and diverse sources of happiness, disasters are, by their nature, destabilizing. Hardships can't be prevented, nor can the unpleasant states caused by them. You can only control how well you prepare, potentially decreasing the length and intensity of your own suffering. Only so much can be done, but it's definitely worth doing.

DO WHAT YOU CAN

This chapter has been an exploration of how mindscaping intersects with the harsher realities of life. Some circumstances are beyond your control. Unexpected natural disasters are inevitable, unpleasant, and, if you're not prepared, severely derailing. Tornadoes can't be stopped, but you can plan in case one strikes. Protecting your happiness and preparing to adapt quickly is prudent. Rebuilding is hard, but it can always be done.

One final note: if you're currently facing a disaster, you should absorb resources beyond this book. This chapter isn't intended as a guide through serious life-altering events. It's only designed to help you reframe when they occur. If you are facing a serious struggle, please find and implement powerful tools specific to your situation.

REFLECTION

The following set of questions is designed to help distill the ideas in this chapter. Take your time answering them and revisit any practices or exercises if you need to.

➜ How well do you handle change? How might you handle it better?

➜ What alternative sources of happiness could you explore?

➜ How do you handle and process emotions?

➜ Who could you reach out to, or what resources could you leverage in a time of need?

➜ What was your most recent natural disaster? How did you work through it?

➜ What areas of your happiness are most vulnerable to natural disaster? How might you reduce this risk?

CONCLUDING THOUGHTS

You made it! That's the entire mindscaping frame-work, caveats and all. This final section contains an overview outlining the process, so you have a quick recap if you're feeling stuck at any time:

→ Imagine an individually owned, alterable landscape as a metaphor for describing the mind.

→ Surveying this landscape creates an understanding of how that mind functions, particularly in regard to thoughts and behaviors.

→ These survey insights can be used to create a vision for your life, resulting in a value-based, happiness-optimizing blueprint.

→ A strong home is critical for undertaking other projects. Confidence and self-esteem underpin all efforts to change your mindscape.

→ Enacting projects requires experimenting with action and system tools. As your experience grows, mindscape changes become easier, shaping them in the direction of your blueprint ideals.

- Mindscape features face erosion and decay over time. As priorities change, it's important to be mindful of how time and energy are split between new projects and maintenance.
- Natural disasters are unexpected, destabilizing life events that damage homes and blueprints. They can be mitigated somewhat, but resilience and re-building are necessary.

IMPROVEMENTS HAPPEN OVER TIME

Mindscaping is a lifelong process. It takes time and effort. Instant, simple solutions would be great, but important life adjustments tend to be more complicated. Mindscapes can be reconstructed for vastly increased happiness, but the shaping process is never done.

No one wakes up one day and thinks, *I'm as happy as possible, and my life will stay this way forever.* Life fluctuates. Permanent equilibrium is never reached. It is, however, possible to wake up and realize, *I experience significantly more happiness than ever before. Life is generally good, and I enjoy it immensely. I have all the tools and frames I need to manage whatever situations life throws at me.* While achievable, it's far from a short, simple journey. This book's purpose lies in creating fundamental improvements in your daily experience, not two-week bursts of idealistic motivation. The process requires a lifetime of effort that is personally paced toward optimization.

....

Progress isn't always instant or linear but accumulates over time. Mindscaping can provide the foundation for constantly improving your life.

....

This framework provides the tools needed to reshape your mind with happiness at the forefront. It contains the concepts for identifying, deconstructing, and reconstructing states and evaluations more desirably. The work must be completed individually, but my hope is that the pathway is now clear.

This resource isn't nearly long enough to address the full complexity of the psyche or every possible way to optimize happiness. That being said, I crafted the book with longevity and universality in mind. While specific tactics may shift due to new research, I expect the overall strategies to remain intact indefinitely. I hope you find them valuable for the entirety of your happiness journey.

TAILOR IT TO YOURSELF

Your mind is unique, so don't be afraid to personalize every component of mindscaping to fit your needs. There is no authoritative path to happiness, and it's likely only some of the practices shared here will fit you personally. While it should be enough to be valuable, it's certainly not the full range of viable pathways. Explore and experiment.

I especially don't expect anyone to zealously follow every strategy, tactic, and word I've written. You should feel confident mixing the information here with your own resources and experiences to craft the best results. Following my approach blindly is against the spirit of this book. Carry forward only what works for you. The intention is to create additional flexibility and control in the way you approach happiness, and ultimately life, not to end up with a carbon copy of my ideas.

START TODAY!

When I read a book like this, a curious thing happens during the last few pages. I blaze through them, excited about implementing the new ideas. I'm hopeful and motivated. Big changes are coming! Until I realize it's already 2 a.m. Alright. Big changes are coming first thing in the morning. For now, sleep.

When morning arrives, I jump out of bed, ready to implement! The morning schedule is tight, though...I'll start after work. Work takes longer than expected. Someone unexpectedly invites me to dinner, which sounds like a nice way to unwind. I accept. Suddenly I'm home and ready for bed: *Wasn't I supposed to work on those personal project ideas? It's pretty late; tomorrow for sure, though.*

Soon, weeks have passed. I've started and finished an entirely different book: *There are some good ideas in here! Oh, wow, is it already 2 a.m.? I better get some sleep. I'm excited to implement these ideas first thing in the morning.* The story repeats itself from here—plenty of consumption, far less execution.

Information is necessary, but change requires action. If you haven't yet, I strongly recommend taking your first step now, before there are any interruptions. Answer one of the previous section's questions or schedule time for reflection or planning. Tell a loved one you want to do an exercise together. Don't put it off until later. Don't do it tomorrow. Take a step now. The very first action is all that's necessary to build momentum, but it's often skipped.

Not sure what to start with? Try a one-minute reflection on your day. What happened? How can you change it for the better? This is a ridiculously small, simple commitment. Do it now and write one action step afterward. Don't move forward until you've done this. Otherwise, the last section won't make sense.

BEST WISHES

Alright, I lied, this section is still coherent, even if you haven't taken action. I just wanted to nudge you toward starting. Congratulations on making it through the entire book! Before closing, I want to express my gratitude for your taking this journey with me. There are a nearly infinite number of ways to spend time, and I'm humbled you chose to invest yours in my book.

I've said plenty for one book. If you'd like to hear more, get in touch, leave feedback, or see my other projects, you can find all my happiness-related projects at www.howtohappy.com. Please reach out. I'd love to hear your stories, experiences, and progress. Thanks again and best of luck!